Mindfulness and Meditation

Ultimate Guide to Achieve Happiness by Eliminating Stress, Anxiety and Depression

(A Simple Way to Using Mindfulness to Boost Positive Thinking)

Paul Zendejas

Published by Rob Miles

© **Paul Zendejas**

All Rights Reserved

Mindfulness and Meditation: Ultimate Guide to Achieve Happiness by Eliminating Stress, Anxiety and Depression (A Simple Way to Using Mindfulness to Boost Positive Thinking)

ISBN 978-1-990084-06-5

All rights reserved. No part of this guide may be reproduced in any form without permission in writing from the publisher except in the case of brief quotations embodied in critical articles or reviews.

Legal & Disclaimer

The information contained in this book is not designed to replace or take the place of any form of medicine or professional medical advice. The information in this book has been provided for educational and entertainment purposes only.

The information contained in this book has been compiled from sources deemed reliable, and it is accurate to the best of the Author's knowledge; however, the Author cannot guarantee its accuracy and validity and cannot be held liable for any errors or omissions. Changes are periodically made to this book. You must consult your doctor or get professional medical advice before using any of the suggested remedies, techniques, or information in this book.

Upon using the information contained in this book, you agree to hold harmless the Author from and against any damages, costs, and expenses, including any legal fees potentially resulting from the application of any of the information provided by this guide. This disclaimer applies to any damages or injury caused by the use and application, whether directly or indirectly, of any advice or information presented, whether for breach of contract, tort, negligence, personal injury, criminal intent, or under any other cause of action.

You agree to accept all risks of using the information presented inside this book. You need to consult a professional medical practitioner in order to ensure you are both able and healthy enough to participate in this program.

Table of Contents

INTRODUCTION 1

CHAPTER 1: WHAT DOES MINDFULNESS MEAN? 4

CHAPTER 2: HOW MINDFULNESS CAN HELP YOU REDUCE STRESS 8

CHAPTER 3: INTRO TO MINDFULNESS 17

CHAPTER 4: THE HISTORY OF MEDITATION 21

CHAPTER 5: WHAT IS MINDFULNESS? 28

CHAPTER 6: INWARD FOCUS 33

CHAPTER 7: MINDFUL CONCENTRATION 36

CHAPTER 8: MINDFULNESS - PRACTICAL STEPS AND EXERCISES 41

CHAPTER 9: COMMUNITY MEDITATION TECHNIQUES 65

CHAPTER 10: HOW MINDFULNESS PLAYS OUT IN EVERYDAY LIFE 80

CHAPTER 11: TIPS TO HARNESS THE POWER OF YOUR OWN SELF WITH MINDFULNESS 85

CHAPTER 12: USING MEDITATION TO IMPROVE SELF-COMPASSION 89

CHAPTER 13: ADVANCED MEDITATION 93

CHAPTER 14: "A SERIES OF BREATHS" 99

CHAPTER 15: MINDFULNESS AT HOME.......................... 106

CHAPTER 16: MINDFULNESS MEDITATION FOR DEEP RELAXATION.. 129

CHAPTER 17: COMMIT TO A REGULAR PRACTICE THAT FEELS NATURAL... 139

CHAPTER 18: HOW TO KNOW WHAT YOU WANT AND GO AFTER IT 143

CHAPTER 19: WHAT IS MINDFULNESS? 150

CHAPTER 20: INTRODUCING THE CONCEPT OF MINDFULNESS.. 174

CONCLUSION... 180

Introduction

There are possibilities that you might have heard of mindfulness meditation and the whole concept of leading a mindful life, but you do not know what it means. You might be fascinated with the idea of attaining greater clarity, focus, awareness, and the greater pace at home, work, or with friends and family, but you are not very sure of how the path looks like to get from one point to another.

You should not worry since everything begins at a certain point. The most important thing is the decision to step onto the path, and because of that bold decision, congratulations are in order. It can really be hard starting on a new journey and attempting to incorporate a new practice in an already moving life. Most of the time, we become unsure of how we are supposed to move on. Especially with something that is as unfamiliar as mindfulness meditation. There are possibilities that you will encounter a number of challenges along the path. For that particular reason, even knowing how to get started can be a big problem. At times, can be easier said than done. Losing dedication and enthusiasm is not uncommon to a new practice, especially when obstacles come up and day-to-day tasks start to get in the way. As you go on, it will be very important to figure out what's working and what's not to enable you to adjust the practice as required. But before you begin the practice of mindfulness, the most important thing would be to understand what the practice could mean for you in your pursuits of personal development.

The main aim of this eBook is to assist you on your path towards a more conscientious, peaceful, and mindfulness life. It will also assist you to achieve greater degrees of satisfaction with your entire life. It is also important to note that the primary aim of this mindfulness meditation eBook is not to change your life someday in the future but to make the impact right now. Once you have learned how to settle, the next thing you should do is to adopt the non-judgmental practice and live in the present. By doing that, you will find yourself at a greater peace with the current circumstance that you are undergoing. With time, striving will begin to fall away, and in its place, you will gain a deep fulfillment that will last with you for the longest time ever.

You should feel free to read this eBook with expectations of changing your life for the better. Again, congratulations for deciding to embark on this great path. This is a journey that will last a lifetime. Of most importance is getting started on a journey that is considered by many as mission impossible.

There are several books and articles on the issue. We are glad you chose to read this one. We have included as much information as we could get on the subject and hope that the book will educate and empower you. Enjoy!

Chapter 1: What Does Mindfulness Mean?

The concept of mindfulness can be defined as a complete and absolute focus on the present. The focus is intentional and it is made without any judgment, as the person pays attention to the present feelings and thoughts. As a beginner into the world of mindfulness, you will soon discover that meditation can help you embrace this concept and discover its advantages. As for the history of mindfulness, it should be mentioned that this concept is derived from the Buddhist practices. Today, it has gone a long way from the original concept, being used in a wide range of countries (including Western countries) for the proper handling of emotions.

Given the fact that mindfulness has become a common practice in Western countries, it should come as no surprise that it has started to be used for the alleviation of varied medical conditions. Psychologists have started to recommend mindfulness as a practice outside the formal setting, treating successfully conditions such as: OCD (obsessive-compulsive disorder), anxiety disorder, mood disorders (depression) and even addiction (drug-related).

As it was mentioned above, the concept of mindfulness is derived from the Buddhist practice and specifically from the element known as 'anapanasati'. In general, the term 'sati' makes reference to the mind being focused on the present and not on the past, as it usually happens. Also, 'sati' is related to the concept of 'recollection', being connected in this way to the future.

Meditation is an essential and intricate part of the mindfulness concept, with both formal and informal practices being available. Those who practice mindfulness are also invited to discover the non-meditation based exercises, such as the mindful tasting of a cherry or other piece of fruit. Formal meditation makes reference to the training of the mind to concentrate on the present; thus, one's attention is derived towards the bodily sensations that are currently experienced, including the breathing. The concept of mindfulness will teach you to concentrate on the moment and everything that arises during that moment. The informal practice of mindfulness will allow you to apply this concept in everyday life, while the non-meditation based exercises are commonly used by psychologists, in behavioral therapy.

If one was to use three words to describe the concept of mindfulness, those three words would be: 'moment', 'awareness' and 'acceptance'. When you choose to apply the concept of mindful attention, you will become more aware of everything that happens in the present, including your thoughts, feelings and bodily sensations. The importance of acceptance is essential for a successful understanding of the mindfulness concept; you will learn to concentrate on your present thoughts and feelings, without necessarily diving them into right and wrong. This can be perceived as a process of training your brain; you are practically teaching your brain to sense what it happens in the moment, instead of constantly relating to the experiences of the past. It is the kind of liberating experience that you will not have the opportunity to experience in any other way; it will teach you how to handle your emotions, without falling prey to the previous negative experiences you had to go through at some point in your life.

Chapter 2: How Mindfulness Can Help You Reduce Stress

The Scourge of Modern Life
Chances are, if you are reading this right now you have access to electricity, an internet connection and a smartphone.
You live in the industrialised world and have been affected by stress at some point in your life.
Stress in modern times is unavoidable.
It is the frontier for worry and anxiety, reflecting the conditions our ancestors faced on the plains of the Savannah centuries ago.
The mention of stress has found its way into everyday use, teenagers now use the term to describe rising stress levels studying for mid-term exams.
But are we stressed or feigning the symptoms to drawn attention to our struggles?

One thing is certain, stress is real. Yet how your body interprets it varies from person to person.

In fact, your tolerance for stress is different to a trained Navy Seal soldier. Yet, we can all agree, when pushed beyond our stress point, our health declines.

The good news is, we can use mindfulness to help us navigate the torrents of stress and manage our lives better.

Mindfulness means paying attention in a particular way; with purpose, in the present moment, and non-judgementally.

It helps you cope with life's challenges by being present and inhabiting your body with attentiveness. This is in contrast to runaway thoughts which pass through your mind without your conscious awareness.

"Mindfulness - the steady, non-judgmental awareness and acceptance of experience - leads to self-awareness and to shifts in our perspectives that allow us to see clearly what's happening and how we are reacting, to respond to triggers and traumas with far more open-mindedness, and to face the process of necessary change with far more flexibility and tolerance," affirm author Linda Graham MFT in, Bouncing Back: Rewiring Your Brain for Maximum Resilience and Well-Being.

Lurking Beneath Surface

Practising mindfulness can help you reduce stress because it shifts your autonomic nervous system from a stressed state to a calm state.

As you are reading this, there are minor stresses taking place in the background you are unaware of, yet your subconscious mind is attentive to.

Stress is insidious. It lurks beneath the surface and strikes when you least expect it, carrying with it accumulated stress from the past which can tip you over the edge.

I liken it to a sequinned pearl necklace, cut at one point and left to unravel into pieces. Stress has the same effect causing life to crumble if left untreated.

Mindfulness can help you cope with the habitual patterns of thinking that dominate your everyday life.

"The practice of mindfulness - training the brain to focus its attenn and to strengthen conscious awareness - allows us to see our conditioned patterns of response clearly so that we can get unstuck from them when we need to," avows Linda Graham MFT.

Mindfulness helps you notice the stream of thoughts passing through your mind moment to moment.

It is a means to check in with yourself to notice what is taking place beneath the surface of your thoughts.

You may be prone to reacting to external conditions, yet seldom take the time to note your emotional well-being. It is often too late when you sense something because an emotional crisis has occurred.

Your thoughts can pull you into the past, where you re-experience uninviting events.

You are not present, but recalling a mental screenplay taken place long ago.

This becomes a stressor because you bring unresolved emotions into your interactions with others, contaminating the beauty of the present moment.

"But any time you let your thoughts, worries, and stresses dictate how you experience this moment, you inevitably suffer, because you're in conflict with reality, with truth. Rather than dancing with life, you're in a wrestling match-and the outcome of the struggle isn't in doubt," declares author Hugh G. Byrne in, The Here-and-Now Habit: How Mindfulness Can Help You Break Unhealthy Habits Once and for All.

Carving Out Time for Silence

Mindfulness can go a long way when you devote regular time for silence.

This is attained through meditation and the sensations created in the body.

Meditation anchors your mind to the present moment, so you become attentive to your present moment experience.

It is important not to fight your thoughts or add a commentary to what you feel, but allow yourself to connect with your feelings.

As you become comfortable sitting in silence, you may wish to advanced your practice via structured meditation. This is ideal to strengthen your knowledge and take you into a deeper meditative state.

The benefits of meditation allow you to detach from your thoughts. You become a silent witness and less invested in the stream of activity created in the mind.

You are less reactive because you interact with what is taking place before you.

Stress abounds because people believe their thoughts.

So, if you are driving home after a hostile encounter with your boss or colleague, and an inconsiderate motorist cuts you off in traffic, you offer them a piece of your mind.

Yet, by practising mindfulness you become attuned to the physical sensations of anger before you retaliate since you are mindful of your emotional state.

Linda Graham MFT affirms, "Mindful awareness - observing and reflecting - allows us to step back from the experience of the moment and observe it from a larger field of awareness that is not any of those experiences, that is larger than any of those patterns. With that awareness, we can begin to see different possibilities for responding."

Mindfulness has a positive effect on your relationships. Your emotional well-being is enriched, instead of succumbing to external stimuli.

The success of mindfulness-based stress reduction lies in noting your thoughts non-judgmentally, through the eyes of equanimity and compassion.

In doing so, you recognise thoughts pass through the landscape of your mind and they needn't turn into negative emotions.

We are heavily invested in our thoughts and have a negativity bias when challenged. This is an evolutionary mechanism to help us make sense of our environment.

So, when thoughts, feelings or sensations emerge, don't ignore them or suppress them, nor analyse or judge them.

Note them as they occur and observe them intentionally but non-judgmentally, moment by moment, in your field of awareness.

If your mind wanders say to yourself, "wandering" and bring your mind back to the present moment.

If you wish to be happy and live a peaceful life, be mindful of your thoughts before they lead you down a perilous path.

Stressful thoughts are not the source of your happiness, but a by-product of unconscious thinking left to run wild.

Mindfulness helps you to reduce stress because it anchors you to the present moment where your body inhabits.

Chapter 3: Intro To Mindfulness

Intro to Mindfulness

Mindfulness involves being aware of your mind and your surroundings during each moment. It means stepping back from making an immediate response and taking a moment to understand how you think and feel. Mindfulness requires you to pay attention to both the world around you and yourself. It teaches you to experience the world instead of only witnessing what happens.

Mindfulness can break down into a variety of components:

1. Attentiveness - Learning to notice what goes on around you. Examples include, feeling the texture of a table with your hand or feeling your heartbeat in your chest.

2. Remaining In The Moment - Learning to live in the present, aware that you have no ability to change your past and

understanding that the future hasn't been written. Your feelings and thoughts are valid and valuable because they occur during the moment.

3. Compassion - Learning to show compassion allows us to recognize our own fallibility and limitations. It allows us to show understanding and forgiveness for others and yourself. We often fall into the trap of succumbing to our negative feeling and thoughts about ourselves and others.

4. Becoming Non-Judgmental - Learning to be aware of things without automatically judging them as good or bad. Awareness of the whole situation gives you the ability to take the appropriate action.

5. Becoming Non-Reactive - Learning to hold off on reacting from a situation as it happens. This doesn't mean not reacting. It means taking a moment to experience and assess the moment that is happening around you. Being able to control your reaction and emotions will give you the ability to properly assess and respond to

situations instead of reacting purely out of emotion.

Benefits of Mindfulness

There are many benefits associated with practicing a mindful lifestyle. These benefits have been extensively researched and have years of data to back up all of their beneficial claims.

1. Focus - Gaining an enhanced ability to focus and suppress distracting information. Mindfulness has been proven to correlate with cognitive flexibility and better attentional functioning.

2. Stress Reduction - Mindfulness has been shown to alleviate stress. Daily mindfulness can aid in decreasing long-term stress and anxiety. It can also alter the cognitive processes in your brain.

3. Negative Thinking Reduction - Mindfulness can help to reduce negative thoughts and decrease rumination. People practicing mindfulness exhibit fewer signs of depression.

4. Improved Memory Function - Mindfulness can substantially boost the amount of working memory over time.

5. Improved Relationships - Practicing mindfulness leads to a positive correlation in relationship satisfaction. When you're mindful, you're less likely to cave in to stress and react negatively toward other people. Mindfulness gives you the necessary tools to better communicate your emotions to others. Mindfulness can also help protect you from giving in to the stressful effects of conflict that arise in any relationship.

6. Less Reaction to Emotions - Mindfulness gives you the ability to be self-observant. It allows you to handle stress and negative situations without letting your emotions rule over you and dictate your actions.

Besides these mindfulness benefits listed above, mindfulness can also give you the ability to modulate your fear, improve your sense of morality, and allow you to act with more intention. The many benefits of being more mindful are well worth the amount of effort and time you put into practicing it.

Chapter 4: The History Of Meditation

Before Common Era (BCE)
Meditation has been around for thousands of years. Exactly when it started is unknown. Archaeologists have found artifacts that support evidence of other scholars to suggest it has been practiced, in one form or another, for around 5,000 years. Its origins were always based in religious practices. But today in the west many people who practice meditation have no real interest in its religious connotations, but purely in its ability to significantly improve their wellbeing.

1,500 BCE. The first records to document meditation were found in India and stem from the Hindu religion. They are from the teachings of "The Vedas."

600 to 500 BCE. Buddhist meditation began in China and India. Buddhist meditations exact origins are unknown but are believed to link back to the Sutras of the Pali Canon.

400 BCE to 100 BCE. The philosophy of yoga, meditation and spirituality called the "Bhagavad Gita," and the outline for the eight limbs of yoga, recorded in The Yoga Sutras of Patanjali, were written.

By 20 BCE in the west, Philo of Alexandria had written meditation like concentration exercises.

Common Era (CE)

2 CE. Plotinus developed a formed meditative technique.

5 CE. The early concept of Zen came to central China from Bodhidharma and the first original school was founded in East Asia by Zhivi.

6 CE. Buddhism was promoted in Korea by Wonhyo and Uisang.

Meditative practices are seen also in Judaism. In the Torah, Isaac is said to "lasuach" in the field. This is believed to be a form of meditative practice. There are further references throughout the Hebrew Bible that Judaism has meditative traditions central to its teachings.

7 CE Japanese Buddhism grew and the meditative practices developed.

600 CE. Dosho, a Japanese monk, learned about Zen while visiting China in 653 CE. When he arrived back in Japan, he opened the first meditation hall at Nara.

1000 to 1100 CE. In the Islamic religion, the remembrance of God is known as "Dhikr" and incorporated in meditative techniques. Specific meditative techniques are found in the practice of Sufism, which appeared in the 11th and 12th centuries. This includes the repetition of holy words and breathing control.

1200 CE. Zazen, a form of meditation that was used by Japanese monks. The concept arrived from China when the Japanese monk Dogen returned from a visit there.

By the Middle Ages, Jewish meditation had grown and changed. The practice had developed and now included meditative approaches to prayer and study.

In Eastern Christian religion, a specific posture and the repetition of a phrase is often involved in meditation. Between the 10th and 14th century, in the byzantine period, the Hesychasm tradition was created. It is a method of meditation that requires looking inward and ceasing to register the senses.

In contrast, Western Christian meditation does not involve any special posture or repetition of phrases. It is a progression of the divine reading called "Lectio Divina" and was read among Benedictine monks in the 6th century. In the 12th century, a monk called Guigo II defined a meditative process based on a "ladder" of four steps: Read, ponder, pray and contemplate. It was developed further by saints in the 16th century, Ignatius of Loyola and Teresa of Avilain.

In the 18th Century, translations of the ancient teachings of Buddhism first landed on western shores. In the 1890s, new schools of yoga were developed by gurus such as Vivekananda.

Siddhartha, which tells the story of Buddha's spiritual journey, was published by Hermann Hesse in 1922.

In 1927, the Book of the Dead, a famous Tibetan book about Buddhism, was published. It attracted westerners towards the teachings of Buddhism.

Insight meditation called The Vipassana started in Burma in the 1950s.

A book called The Dharma Bums by Jack Kerouac was first published in 1958. It attracted a lot of interest and sparked curiosity about meditation.

New types of meditation began appearing in the 1960s, including Transcendental Meditation (TM).

The medical world started taking an interest in the effects of meditation and mindfulness when the Mindfulness Centre was opened by Dr. Jon Kabat-Zinn in 1979. He then started the Stress Reduction Program at the University of Massachusetts. It treated patients with chronic illness.

The Chopra Centre for Wellbeing was founded by Dr. Deepak Chopra and Dr. David Simon in 1996.

In 1997, a book entitled The Power of Now: A Guide to Spiritual Enlightenment was published by Eckhart Tolle. It introduced present-moment awareness and tuning into your deepest self through meditation.

Deepak Chopra's book "Spontaneous Fulfilment of Desire" was published in 2003. It highlights using meditation to focus on one's desires and the way to connect to infinite possibilities that exist in everything around us.

The National Centre for Complementary and Alternative Medicine published a study in 2007. Stating that 9.4% of Americans meditated.

By 2012, meditation was becoming mainstream. There were by now groups, teachers, clinics, studios, social meet-ups, retreats and spiritual centers all focusing on meditation, often in combination with yoga, all over America and the western world in general.

On August 8, 2014, over 100,000 people from around the globe came together to take part in the largest meditation gathering in history. It was done to meditate for peace.

Chapter 5: What Is Mindfulness?

Back in the 1960's, a famous psychologist named Fritz Perls used to say, "Lose your mind and come to your senses." This is the essence of mindfulness. Being mindful means being more fully aware of what is around us - what we can see, hear, touch, taste and also what is happening inside us - our thoughts and feelings. We as human beings, are innately gifted and cursed with the ability of being able to look into the future, or think about the past.

Being able to think, plan and envision for the future, or look back into the past and learn from it, is one of the key elements which has allowed us to survive as a species. Think about it. No other known organism can plan or envision their future anywhere near as effective as human beings.

In evolutionary terms, this 'gift' has allowed us to plan ahead and increase our survival and in modern times, it has allowed us to build skyscrapers, technology and achieve personal goals, dreams and aspirations. However, the problem is that most of us simply cannot slow or ease our racing thought processes. We think too much. We are always planning ahead or dwelling on the past which causes; worry, anxiety and panic.

Think about all the sleepless nights you may have had because of the simple fact that your mind was hyperactive. You may have been anxious about school, worrying about relationships, or dwelling on bad experiences in the past. This is the nature of the mind and it can either help us grow or break us down. Optimistic people will have constant positive and uplifting thoughts, while pessimistic people will have continually unproductive and self-destructive thoughts.

Practicing mindfulness allows you to slow down the constant thinking. Mindfulness is simply focusing your awareness on something, anything and fully immersing yourself in the experience of that. Allowing you to fully experience what is occurring in the present moment. It is common to focus on your breathing. Closing your eyes allows you to get rid of any visual distractions which can make your mind wander again.

You may have heard of mindfulness meditation, another form of mindfulness practice. This is where people sit comfortably, close their eyes and begin breathing deeper into their belly. They focus their awareness on their breathing, which allows them to channel their thoughts. Slowly, they begin to focus on other senses; touch, sound, taste, smell and really begin to fully become aware of all that is going on around them, without judgement or ego. The beauty about practicing mindfulness or any form of meditation, is that the more you practice it, the more you 'rewire' your brain to becoming a lot more peaceful and less hectic.

You may have heard of neuroplasticity, the fact that our brains can physically change with new thoughts and experiences. Our brains are like a computer in the sense that the hardware (brain) creates the software (mind). However, the amazing thing about the brain is that the software can actually remodel and alter the hardware. There has been extensive research showing how mindfulness practice can actually 'rewire' our brain by reducing gray matter in regions such as the amygdala (responsible for primitive emotions and fear) and increasing gray matter in regions such as the hippocampus (responsible for memory and learning). Overall, this actually leads to a greater sense of calm, clarity of thought and quality of life.

Mindfulness can be a life-altering practice, because it will help you be in control of your thoughts and emotions. It also has numerous health benefits which we will discuss in following chapters. Mindfulness, just like any other practice, requires continual and consistent effort. You get what you put in, so it's important to try and commit to engaging in a form of mindfulness practice every single day. We will go into the specifics of how to practice mindfulness in the next chapter and other forms of mindfulness practices in following chapters.

Chapter 6: Inward Focus

After posture, the next step in successful meditation is to focus on your inward journey. This step is achieved by focusing on your body—but this time, listening to it in order to achieve the desired state of relaxation necessary for meditation.

Stillness

In your meditation sitting position, pay attention to your body. Try to sit without moving. If your hand or foot wants to shake or twitch, acknowledge this, and then let the urge go. Do not force yourself to be still—rather, settle into it, imagining each twitch or movement is taking the urge to do it away. Feel a calm stillness pervade your body. Once you are peacefully still, it is now time to focus on inner stillness.

Breathing

Breathe through your nose. Pay attention to your breath. Feel your sides and diaphragm coordinate your breath. Focus on how it feels to breathe, allowing your breath to be relaxed and natural, not forced. As you focus, you will find your breathing naturally smooths out and becomes slower and deeper.

Stay with this breathing. It will relax your mind and body, calming your nervous system with each cycle of breathing in and then out. Distracting thoughts should diminish as you prepare your mind to turn inward. Do not fight any thoughts that do come. Acknowledge them, then return your focus to your breath. Feel your mind turning inward as you prepare to meditate.

Relaxation

While you continue to sit in stillness and focus on your breathing, take stock of your body now. Travel with your mind from the top of your head downwards to your feet. In any place you feel tension or unrest, simply imagine those spots softening and relaxing. Now, return from your feet back up to your head, continuing to find and soften any areas of tension.

Chapter Summary: remember the following points each time you prepare to meditate. They will set you up mentally for success:

Stillness

Breathing

Chapter 7: Mindful Concentration

Mindfulness brings about joy and happiness through increased concentration. Mindfulness carries the seed of concentration within it. When you become aware of something you have never paid serious attention to before, something such as a beautiful flower and its beautiful smell, you concentrate on that particular flower at that very moment. Your concentration becomes powerful when your mindfulness becomes powerful. The moment you gain full concentration, you acquire the power to gain deeper insight into anything around you and life generally.

For instance, concentrating on something such as the clouds and the mysteries behind their formation and existence can give you deeper insight into the nature of the clouds. Further, when you meditate on something such as a beautiful piece of rock, you can see into the beautiful and unique nature of that rock as well as the energies embedded in it. If you choose to concentrate on any particular individual, you can understand the full nature of that person. You can even turn your meditation and concentration efforts onto yourself as a way to understand yourself better and learn the cause of formation and triggers of your anger, anxiety, fear, worry, peace, happiness, etc.

With your increased mindfulness and the concentration it brings, you will enjoy life and all of its beauties more. When you concentrate on the sun as it rises or sets, the sun will reveal its true beauty to you.

Take an instance where your spouse offers you a sweet cup of your favorite tea with its sweet and alluring aroma. If you do not concentrate on the tea, you cannot enjoy its true taste and aroma. On the other hand, when you concentrate on it, you enjoy all of its beauty and enjoy the stimulating effect it has on your taste buds.

How to Practice Mindful Concentration

Here is how to practice mindful concentration:

Learn to concentrate on your breath first and follow each cycle of breath through to the end. Use the mindful breathing exercise discussed in the previous section. Once you can concentrate on your breaths, you can concentrate on anything.

Deal with interruptions as things that do not matter. For instance, while meditating, if you hear a loud bang outside and get scared into alertness, acknowledge the sound, and simply return to your breaths. If you suddenly remember you forgot to shut the door, turn off the TV or light bulb, acknowledge the thought, and simply refocus on the breathing. This way, you become your breath.

As you repeatedly succeed at concentrating on your breaths, your breaths will naturally become slower and deeper, more peaceful and harmonious.

You can then translate this mindfulness and increased concentration to whatever tasks you have lined up after the meditation session such as doing your laundry, dishes, cleaning your home, bathing, doing your manicure/pedicure, walking your pet, getting your kids ready for school, eating breakfast, talking with your spouse or colleague, driving to work, etc.

As your level of concentration increases through improved mindfulness, you will start noticing beautiful landscapes you have always ignored as you drive to work, beautiful colleagues and their great dress sense, or haphazardly placed working equipment around the workplace.

Food will suddenly begin to taste better. You will start noticing all the small sacrifices and efforts your partner makes to keep the relationship working. With this increased concentration, you will start paying more attention to your job roles, enjoying them while on them, and because your concentration will have improved, you will be able to overlook distraction and do more each day. The feeling of joy and peace this brings compares to none.

Chapter 8: Mindfulness - Practical Steps And Exercises

The Buddha said that we become what thoughts we have. He said that if the mind is pure, joy will follow and never leave. These wise words of Buddha, spoken nearly 2500 years ago are perhaps more relevant today than they were two millennia ago!

To overcome negativity in our lives we must surround ourselves with positive people and experiences. We must overcome even the greatest obstacle we face towards happiness - our own thoughts. Strangely enough, our thoughts are among the few things in our lives that are within our control. Due to our lifestyle, we lose the ability to master our thoughts or at the very least our ability is dulled much in the same way a knife becomes dull with continued use. Using the proper meditation techniques, we can sharpen those dull edges and regain control of how and what we feel and actively direct our thoughts.

The steps explained below do not in any way substitute treatment required for serious mental conditions. Individuals undergoing clinical or therapeutic treatment for emotional disturbances are advised to check with their physician or psychologist prior to starting this alternative therapy. This is only a layman's guide to get a brief insight into this remarkable practice. If this book inspires you, professional guidance can be availed for a more in-depth understanding of mindfulness meditation.

Here we go!

The practice of Mindfulness has three components:

Formal mindfulness

Informal mindfulness

Non-meditative exercises.

<u>Formal mindfulness.</u> As the name suggests, this is the formal practice of

mindful meditation. It involves choosing a quiet time and place to give yourself to the practice of focusing on the breath and body sensations as and when they occur. For the beginner the traditional meditation poses may not be comfortable although you may attempt the cross-legged position. If you find that difficult, you may sit in a chair with your feet flat on the floor. With closed eyes, one travels inwards concentrating first on the breath.

If practicing mindfulness could be seen as having a meal, then **formal mindfulness** would be the entrée and the heartiest part of the fare and **informal mindfulness** and **non-meditative exercises** would be the appetizer and dessert portions of the meal. The one is anchored by the other two and they all complement each other to nourish and satisfy the diner. Similarly, the formal practice will be that regularly scheduled session that will provide the most benefit and the other two components will support and re-inforce the advances made in this area. Each component complements the others and works together to help you to connect the ever more frequent incidents of mindfulness until it becomes a way of life.

Let us move on to the other components and then return to an in-depth discussion of formal mindfulness.

Informal mindfulness. This involves no specific place or posture. The same mindful concentration is adopted on and off or continuously throughout the day. It is an especially good way to start your initiation into mindfulness as some may find it difficult to start with formal mindful meditation.

Regular mundane activities are ideal for informal practice. Start by choosing a particular action like brushing your teeth, which is done without much thought. Pay complete attention to your action and count the brush strokes. Here you are mindful about your actions which are taking place at that moment and you sustain those thoughts until the action is completed. Do this every time you brush your teeth and follow the practice for a week. Then the following week, choose another routine activity and be mindful about it – it can be something as mundane as preparing a daily meal, give it your entire attention and do not allow your thoughts to stray. Your entire being is involved in that activity and in that moment. Until you begin to do this, you may not realize how frenetic your thoughts are. Different studies place the thoughts that pass through our minds at between 42 and 48 thoughts per minute. Focusing completely on one task develops that discipline of being wholly present.

Diligent practice of informal mindfulness will immediately begin to yield the positive benefit of an improved quality of life. Once you have learnt the technique of channelling inner peace through the formal meditative practice, persistence in the informal practice will be easy. This is because you will notice the positive impact and this will reinforce your desire to strive for it. Your response to any difficult situation in your life will be mindful, that is to say, a detached, non-judgmental, non-reactive response. This is not to say that you will lose any of your decisiveness or ability to address problems, but you will have the ability to reframe the problem in your mind and your response will likely be more effective. This is termed a 'relaxation response' as opposed to the 'stress response' which is your normal reaction.

Let us understand this through an example. As a Type A individual you are usually very diligent at your tasks, you may not necessarily like to rely on other team members for your outcomes (remember those dreaded group assignments in high school and college!). Say your VP assigns a project to a team of four and you get together and come up with an action plan. When you have done all that you are required to do and possibly more but the task falls short because someone else failed to perform, doesn't that frustrate you? It is enough to push some folks over the proverbial edge. In the face of your boss' disappointment, immediately your body shifts into panic mode. You feel your heart rate increase; your throat feels constricted, maybe perspiration forms on your brow. This is the stress response. You may want to 'out' your colleague(s) right there and then, and perhaps end up saying or doing something which you will later regret. Now is the time to switch gears. Shift your thoughts to the inner peace that you are starting to cultivate. Take a few deep breaths and focus your attention to your body and breathing. Maybe listen to your breath traversing the nasal passage on its way out. Gradually you will feel the stress which was building up, start to ease. After a while you can look at the situation like a detached observer and make the appropriate decision. Who knows, you may decide to expose your team mate(s) after all, but it will definitely be a decision that you made and not one your explosive emotions caused you to stumble into.

It may be helpful to have some pre-determined 'if/then' responses to help you with your natural tendency to grow impatient, restless or aggressive. These are responses that you will default to when you find yourself becoming stressed or uptight. Whether you are running late in bumper to bumper traffic or navigating the sometime landmine territory of a romantic relationship, informal mindfulness is readily available to you. Attaining this degree of concentration comes after much practice but soon you will be able to slip easily into informal mindfulness as the need arises.

<u>Non-meditative exercises</u>. This involves being mindful and aware of the moment when an action is being done. Throughout the day, be mindful of the things you do. For example, if you are chewing on a piece

of fruit, be mindful of the sensations the experience arouses. Take it all in and then move on.

If you have had no prior experience with mindfulness practices or meditation, it is good to start with non-meditative exercises and then move to informal mindfulness and then to formal mindful meditation. Remember that it takes some practice to get into the habit of mindfulness. Do not be disheartened if you are unable to do so in the first few sessions. For the untrained mind, the challenge is to quiet the racing mind in order to achieve focus. The ancient meditation writings likens the mind to a monkey jumping around from one tree to the next and that is truly what you will discover when you begin the journey to mindfulness. Just as in the learning of a new art or skill, be determined in your pursuit and it will yield results.

Once you have advanced into the formal practice, you will realize that one practice underpins the others. We may not be able to practice formal mindfulness for extended periods throughout our regular day so the informal practice helps us to sustain the benefits in our regular activities.

Getting Started

Choose a comfortable location for your meditation session. An ideal spot should not be too brightly lit or have such bright and vivid colors that it is distracting. Choose a space and time when you anticipate no disturbances for the duration of the time you plan to meditate. You will also want to have control over any ambient noises like the television. If you find that it helps you to relax, you may play some soft music in the background although you will want to be cautious that it doesn't create a distraction.

Wear comfortable clothing that allows you to relax and feel at ease for an extended period. Be aware of the temperature of the area and dress accordingly to avoid discomfort should it become too cold or warm after sitting for a while. A feeling of unease will pull your thoughts away again and again and will only defeat the purpose to be achieved.

Choose a posture that is comfortable for you. Although some people who have meditated for a long time will tell you that the ideal posture is being seated in the traditional lotus position, it is certainly not where they began their journey. Below I have included illustrations of variations of the sitting posture depending on your ease and comfort. You may place your legs folded one over the other in the lotus or half-lotus pose. You can also sit in the customary cross-legged position being careful to maintain a straight back. You can even choose to kneel as you meditate.

Figure 1 - LOTUS

Figure 2 - HALF LOTUS

-

Figure 3 - CROSS LEGGED

Figure 4 – KNEELING

If none of these poses seem comfortable to you, you can try the standing pose with feet slightly apart and weight equally distributed on both feet. Imagine yourself literally rooted to the ground beneath you. Let your arms hang limp at your sides. Do a gentle shake of your arms and body to rid yourself of any existing tension and stand with legs bent slightly at the knees.

Another posture is the reclining pose. Lie on your right side with the right hand placed under the head and the left arm resting along the body on the left side. A small soft pillow may be used for comfort. This is also called the lion pose. Always pay close attention to your body – if you find the position affects your breathing or circulation, modify it. I usually recommend avoiding the corpse posture (lying on your back) at the outset because it may induce sleep.

You can also meditate while in a seated position. Choose a straight-backed chair where you can sit comfortably but without resting on the back of the chair. Your back should be straight but not rigid – shrug your shoulders and take some deep breaths to start in order to ensure that your back, shoulders and abdomen are relaxed. Your feet should be flat on the floor and you may place your hands on the knees with your palm facing up.

We will examine four different aspects of Mindfulness that is particularly helpful to the Type A personality.

Mindfulness in Body

Close your eyes and take some deep breaths to relax yourself. You should begin to experience a sense of calm. Bring awareness to your body in an exercise designed to notice or observe each part of the body. Body scanning may start at the head and move downward or at the toes and move upward. The direction is not important but once you have decided on your methodology, stick with it so it becomes easier and more natural with practice. To understand the concept of body scanning, imagine a document scanner as the shaft of light moves from one end to the next recording the text or image progressively as the light moves along it. This is what you will be doing – you will be mentally exploring each individual body part in sequence and observing any sensations as they become evident. At this point there is no need to make judgments about how you feel, you are merely an observer.

If you were to start with your toes, be aware of any physical sensations whether of pain, discomfort, warmth, tightness or the lack of any sensation at all and gradually move upwards bringing the same amount of attention and awareness to your lower legs then upper legs, hips, buttocks, pelvis, stomach, chest, your lower back, upper back, shoulders, upper arms, lower arms, hands fingers, neck, face. Feel free to linger on each part noting the sensations that arise, and dispel any tension that you find. It may be helpful for you to consider the scan as you giving loving and gentle attention to each of your body parts providing each one with whatever it needs in that moment.

If this seems challenging for you, you can explore the option of registering for guided body scanning sessions. Mindfulness is widely practiced and you are almost certain to find a local meditation center that can help. You can also find videos online with guided sessions to get you familiar with how scanning works and to get you started.

As your mind and body become more closely aligned through this practice, you will be able to exercise more control over how you react to stressful situations. Going back to that example of the failed work task that caused Mr. Type A to experience a characteristic stress response – being familiar with body scanning, he could quickly identify within his body where the sensation of tension or stress is centered and be deliberate about giving the same loving, **mindful** attention to those areas to relax them and calm himself down. He would immediately begin to feel the heat of the moment dissipating allowing him to be more rational in his reaction.

Listening to our bodies is important, too often we are consumed with activities and we expect our bodies to acquiesce to our demands without being aware of the subtle messages they may be transmitting.

Being present and mindful regarding our bodies will attune us to pick up the signals of fatigue or tension and maybe even early signs of more chronic problems that require our attention.

Mindfulness of Thought

As always begin your session by focusing on the breath in order to calm yourself. Bring your attention to your thoughts, dreams, ideas, fantasies and mental images. Mindfulness in this instance is observing your thoughts or the wanderings of your mind in a detached way. There are several visualization methods that are suggested for this exercise. You may consider your thoughts to be leaves drifting along with the flow of the river as you observe from the river's edge. Your thoughts could be waves in the ocean just coming and going, one always being replaced by another in a constant flow. You can also envision your thoughts as clouds in the sky drifting by – perhaps linked to my childhood fascination with clouds – this is my favorite method to achieve mindfulness of thought. The important thing to remember here is that you are observing your thoughts and not engaging with them. You are not required to judge them or react to them in any way. You simply note the thoughts as they drift by. You can label them as they pass – 'sadness', 'annoyance', 'joy' – note what the thought represents, whether they are connected to each other, if they lead into each other or if they enter your realm of consciousness seemingly on their own. You may also consider whether there are external triggers that prompt these thoughts or do they arise due to how much concentration they are given.

This exercise is eye-opening for many because for the first time you will become aware of how chaotic thought patterns can be. It can also give insight into how easily someone with Type A tendencies can become mentally exhausted with their inclination towards control in all areas of their lives. Ironically, this exercise does help with that Type A tendency towards control and perfection. By detaching yourself from your thoughts, you create a space for yourself that can be very liberating. Much in the same way that the older you can now look back and see mistakes that you made in the past which were not so obvious back then, disengaging from your active thoughts allows a wiser version of yourself to emerge and to then be able to help you with present-day issues.

If you find that you struggle in your personal relationships, an exercise that may be helpful for you is to observe and make note of your 'judgment' thoughts. Type A's can be quite rigid in their standards – they have high expectations of themselves **and others**. This can lead to a hypercritical and judgmental way of thinking that makes for challenging relationships. No-one wants to feel constantly judged or to live in the shadow of another's disapproval. By detaching yourself and observing these negative thoughts, you can decide whether some adjustment may be required on your part to bring healing to your relationships or at the very least improve on them.

Mindfulness of Emotions

This practice involves bringing your focus to your feelings. Are you angry or happy? Peaceful or anxious? Worried or calm? Zero in on your current state of mind and explore it fully. Emotions are dynamic in that they begin with an initial reaction but then they can translate into sensations in the body, then thoughts that prompt action. Everything that plays out from the time we begin to feel the emotion, any triggers, thoughts or resulting actions can be dissected and observed with heightened awareness. Training the mind to take a step back and watch emotional reactions as they occur may serve a 'hot-headed' Type A very well. The sooner you begin to identify patterns and triggers, the less likely you will be to respond impulsively or rashly.

Bringing awareness to your emotions is not only applicable to negative emotions. You want to observe yourself in every scenario, it may even be helpful to make note of your emotions over a period of time. You can record how you feel, what are the accompanying sensations in your body, what are your thoughts, what would you like to do, what **do** you do. By observing and recording your emotions without judgment, you will find that you begin to accept yourself, warts and all, more than you ever have. The practice of mindfulness creates opportunities for us to be more compassionate with ourselves and even extend that grace to others.

Our emotions are a natural part of our makeup – they are neither good nor bad in of themselves – they are merely signals to us and they need to be managed well. By being aware of your emotions and your 'tipping point', you can begin to manage your responses even before entering the situation; and when the situation does arise, you can respond with compassion, gentleness, patience and a willingness to compromise.

There is a correlation between our mental consciousness and the thoughts that we have. If the mental state is one of tiredness, the thoughts could be depressing. If the mental state is energetic, the thoughts will be happy. If it is in an aroused state of excitement, then thoughts may be flighty and hard to control. With practice, one can master how to gently bring in compassion to alter depression, calmness when angry and appreciation to counter dissatisfaction.

Acquiring the skill of self-control in managing emotions is key to the success of the individual with Type A tendencies. Mindfulness can deliver the results that you seek but it requires practice and commitment. Some helpful practices may be:

Introduce affirmations into your daily practice to reinforce the positive way that you plan to deal with conflicts and disagreements even when your emotions are screaming the opposite.

Be kind to yourself – make sure to schedule in adequate rest and recreation to avoid a relapse.

Maintain a gratitude journal. Being thankful makes it very difficult for you to hold on to negative emotions.

Chapter 9: Community Meditation Techniques

Nothing compares to a face-to-face connection that allows you to share ideas and get the satisfaction that we yearn for. We need to look for a community meditation center that allows you to meditate in a group.

So, why is it ideal to meditate with others?

Meditation Is Better When Shared

Just like anything and everything else, things are better when you share them among many people. It is like music that you can't enjoy alone. Well, you can dance to the song alone, but you won't dance for all that long. When you meditate, you can create a connection with other practitioners by tapping into the silence as well as the source of the peace at the same time.

Studies show that when you meditate as a group, you will be able to synchronize your brainwaves the best way.

Helps Develop Your Habit

Many people look for excuses so that they don't meditate at home. Some say that the kids disturb them while others don't have the strength to meditate for a whole session. Meditating in the house also requires you to be fully motivated, which means getting a meditation group will help you stay motivated for long.

When you work in a group, you develop a habit such that you become consistent in all that you do.

You Get feedback on What You Do

A community of meditation practitioners usually include people that are at different meditation levels. If you have just started meditation, you might get other members to help clear any form of confusion.

The other practitioners will help to understand and handle other forms of meditation and help you find answers to address difficulties in the practice.

When you meditate in a group, you also get feedback on what you do and what you don't do. If you do something well, you will get immediate feedback on it, and if you do something bad, you will also get feedback on it.

You Become a Part of a Bigger Picture

A group can support your journey towards inner peace better than when you do it individually. You will get inspired and motivated to connect with other people that share the intentions for inner peace and world peace as well.

It is much better to be part of the change you desire to see in the world when you are part of a team. You will be able to identify and add strengths to your intentions.

More Power in Numbers

Studies show that there is a ripple effect when you are surrounded by people that you get to meditate together

Spiritual Support is Stronger

Just the way you meet with your friends each day when you meditate in a group you get to create a form of synergy that is seen as a connection of two or more parts so that you can achieve something bigger than when you do things on your own.

Additionally, the healing power of meditation is far much powerful than meditating on your own.

Even when you have the best intentions, maintaining a steady daily practice can be a huge challenge. This is why you need to work with others so that you jumpstart and maintain the practice. When you meditate in a group, you get the chance to keep on meditating, whether you do it each day or weekly.

Additionally, you are less likely to give up when you meditate in a group.

You Get the Right Form of Support

When you talk to others, and they share their meditation experience with you, you realize that you aren't alone in a predicament. You get to experience the challenges as well as the joys of meditation in the right way. When you feel like giving up, you can look at the challenges that other people are facing and then realize that you aren't going through a hardship alone.

Enjoy Compassion

When you share your problems with other people, you make them look easier to handle compared to when you do it on your own. The people around you will make it easier for you to understand that things will go bad at times, but they won't always be bad all the time. When you share your experiences with other people, you get to rest in the understanding as well as the kindness that is shown by the other people.

Group Meditation Tips

For you to enjoy the various benefits that arise from group meditation, you need to follow a few tips. Failure to follow some tips ends up making the group boring and less focused.

Effective group meditation works well when each practitioner shares the overall responsibility of creating the perfect atmosphere of peace. Let us look at some tips that will help you enjoy the benefits that a group offers.

Arrival

Make sure that you arrive at the venue on time. It is usually prudent that you arrive a few minutes before the session starts so that you prepare and move along with everyone else. Secondly, if you arrive and the meditation is already started, try and be silent when you join in. Don't distract the people already meditating.

Preparation

Before you can join the group, it is just wise that you prepare. First, turn off all the mobile devices that you have come with. Mobile phones are some of the top distractions that you can leave turned on because you don't know whether you left an alarm on or if a message will come in. Remember that any meditation session requires strict compliance with the no-distraction policy.

If you have a cold or a cough, or any condition that might distract others, try and meditate on your own at home or in a different room. If you start coughing or sneezing within the chapel, head to the restroom immediately and find a way to recover before you join in the meditation.

Try and buy clothes specifically meant for meditation. Any slight noise from the rustling of the clothes will make things hard for everyone. Remember that the environment is silent and still, so any slight noise will be detected immediately. The clothes you buy need to be made of soft fabric.

Don't wear strong scents or perfume as this will distract some people, especially those that are sensitive to smell. When you leave the vehicle, make sure you don't carry any food to the chapel. You can carry a bottle of water but try to take a sip only when you have started chanting.

If you have jewelry and bangles, make sure that they don't make any noise when you move any part of your body. It is best that you remove them and put them in your handbag prior to entering the chapel.

During Meditation

You aren't supposed to talk during the session. Try and maintain total silence when seated. If you are pressed, try and wait till the chanting periods before you visit the restroom. If need be, you can stand and stretch gently during the chanting period.

Departure

Try and make sure you stay for the duration of the session. If you cannot handle the whole session, then you can leave at the start of chanting, and maintain silence as you leave the session.

How to Find the Right Meditation Class

The therapist will have various meditation classes that you can join, but you need to understand what suits your personality type as well as your goals. The therapist will give you a list of classes that you can choose from. Unless you have a specific class in mind, you will have to follow a few tips to help you get the best class for your needs.

Let us look at the top tips to help you get what you need.

Experiment

Before you can settle for a single class, it is ideal that you experiment with several. Try to find out what the different meditation classes offer and who runs them before you make a decision.

The best way to identify what suits your needs is to try all the different types and then see what feels great.

Identify the Dominant sense

You need to identify the dominant sense that will help you calm down. Do you feel calm when you undertake mindful meditation, or do you feel calm when you use visualization? What about a body scan or relaxing music? Everyone is different, and when this happens, we usually respond to a different stimulus. Make sure you choose a meditation practice that will highlight your dominant sense rather than one that doesn't give you maximum benefits.

Connect With the Teacher

If you are in a session where the teacher doesn't make you comfortable, leave, and get another teacher for your needs. The teacher that you work with needs to be able to identify what you need and help you go ahead with it.

The teacher shouldn't make you feel distracted and shouldn't take you at a speed that you aren't sure about. At times, it is more about the teacher himself rather than what he is teaching.

Watch Videos

You can watch the various videos on YouTube to identify what to expect when you go for a session. Watch two or more videos touching on every style of meditation that you are after. When you watch the videos, you will get an idea of what style of meditation suit you the best.

Be Consistent

The benefits that come with meditation don't do so overnight; rather, you have to be consistent and put in all the efforts you can muster. For most of the time, try and stay committed to the goals that you have and go after them. Remember that consistency will make the difference between enjoying what the meditation brings and losing out.

Even if you don't think that the style of meditation isn't working for you, continue at it for at least ten more days so that you can make a factual decision. Remember that you need to put a lot of effort into the meditation when you are beginning a new style, which can make it harder for you.

Dedicate the Right Time

You need to come up with the right time to go for group meditation sessions. Have a habit whereby you practice the same thing each day. For instance, if you have trouble sleeping, try and plan an evening meditation session that will calm your mind.

Understand the Benefits

When you start with group meditation, try and understand what you stand to gain before you can start. Once you understand the benefits, take time to adopt the right strategy that will give you all you want. Remember that the benefits come in fast, though you will take some time for you to notice any major changes.

Some of the major benefits of meditation include a higher sense of self, better sleep, you will feel more rested, and you can increase the levels of energy, and your mind becomes clearer.

Just like any other practice, it is hard for you to incorporate meditation into your routine at first. Start small and then grow gradually.

How do you choose the Right Meditation Technique?

We have talked about so many things and forgot about a major aspect of meditation – choosing the right technique. We have discussed so many techniques without understanding how you choose the right technique. Do you know that you have so many techniques that you can choose from, and you might be spoilt for choice. Let us look at the various tips to get you started.

The Enjoyment

You need to go for a technique that is easy to muster and allows you to enjoy what you do. If you have time and you live an easy life, then you can consider a technique that doesn't demand a lot from you.

I f you live on the fast lane, and then consider a technique that is more relaxing and that provides you relaxation from the daily rigors of life.

Effectiveness

The technique that you choose needs to help you achieve your goals. If you have been advised by a therapist that you need to go for meditation in order to make things move for you, and then you need to get a technique that will give you health success.

If you are looking at a technique to help you lose weight, then you need to find one that can do that.

Must Be Practical

You need to choose a technique that is practical for you. If you have all the time in the world, then go for a technique that you can do more time. On the other hand, if you are always short of time, then opt for something that can take a few minutes a day.

Learn the Technique from an Expert

Remember that meditation is an art that has been around for thousands of years. Teaching the technique is more of a transmission rather than a course. The expertise is passed from generation to generation, from teacher to teacher, and so on. The longer the transmission of the information, the greater the power of the final recipient.

Don't Go for Instant Delivery

There are so many skillful and better ways to present meditation to you, but you need to be wary of the people that promise instant gratification from meditation.

You need to understand that meditation takes time and practice, and a lot of effort. It might reach a point whereby the meditation is boring, and when this happens, you need to keep at it because nothing good comes easy. Stay away from meditation packages that promise that you will enjoy the benefits in a few steps, always remember that meditation is not as simple as you think.

Chapter 10: How Mindfulness Plays Out In Everyday Life

Taste and texture

You may be wondering how mindfulness can be practiced in everyday life. It's easy. You can practice mindfulness in most areas of life. For example, when you eat something, how often do you eat it so fast that you don't really remember the texture, the taste, the experience of eating? You may not even remember the aroma, the presentation, how you cut the food or how it was presented. Notice everything. By doing this, you cut out space for negative thought and are able to experience the joy of eating your meal, making it into a complete experience.

All the way through your life, you are presented with opportunities to put mindfulness to work. Here are some ways in which you can use mindfulness, even though you have things to do or places to go.

Housework and routine tasks

You probably do this as a routine and don't give it much thought. While you are cleaning windows, your concentration may be on other things. Try to think of the joy of the moment. As the vacuum runs over the pile of the carpet, be aware of the different ways that the pile moves. While cleaning windows, get immersed in what you are doing. The reason? You are living that moment to the full. You are not allowing past to interfere with your emotions and you are not letting the future worry you. You are simply enjoying the moment.

Observation

Watching without being judgmental is something that takes practice. If you see things that you don't like, then learn acceptance. For example, you may notice someone wearing something you wouldn't spend money on. Observe it, absorb it and then move on. The idea isn't to reinforce negative thoughts or to judge what you like and what you don't like. It's simply being aware of what is happening around you in that set moment in time. Mindfulness isn't judgmental and that's an extremely important rule to remember. It's a hard lesson for people to learn because we have all these set ideas in our heads about what's right and wrong and these stop us from being able to be truly free. If you see something you may have judged as unsuitable for you simply view it as something happening in that moment in time, rather than something that needs you to judge it. Accept that it is. It's really as simple as that, but simplicity isn't always necessarily easy. You need to practice to get good at it.

Listening

Your listening powers are amazing. Being aware of the sounds around us and absorbing them, again without judgment, is very hard. There will be kinds of music that do not appeal to you. If you have the choice, put on music that you like and let your mind absorb it. It isn't a background to that particular moment in time. It **is** that moment in time. Dance among the notes, listen to all of the different instrumentation or the levels and pitches of the voice you are listening to. This kind of mindfulness makes you very aware of the moment and is great practice for those who are unaccustomed to mindfulness methods.

Listening to what someone has to say is equally important. People spend too much time self-absorbed and a lot of misunderstandings occur because people don't really listen to others. When someone is talking to you, pay attention to the words being said, the body language being used and really take in, again without judgment, what they are saying. It makes you a lot more accepting of other people to practice mindfulness in your contact with others. It's not about your opinion. It's about listening to the sounds of the words, noticing what a speaker's eyes are saying, and actually thinking of nothing other than what is being said.

Using all of your senses

Your eyes see some pretty amazing things in every moment that they are awake. From the moment you wake up in the morning, really look at what they are seeing. For example, instead of merely asking what kind of weather it's going to be today, open the curtains and observe. Feel the changes of the seasons, the cold and the warm and accept each for what it is. Each moment of seeing things is a moment of acceptance. Don't criticize or judge, simply observe. Use your sense of smell to notice great aromas and to take in the perfume of the flowers or the aroma of a curry. Use your ears to open up your senses of sound and your sense of touch to feel different textures, softness or solidity.

Chapter 11: Tips To Harness The Power Of Your Own Self With Mindfulness

In order to obtain a calm and focused mind, and reap the benefits of mindfulness, some of the key components to practicing mindfulness successfully are:

● Focus on your thoughts. Your mind will wander constantly but try to focus on what you want to think about. Focus on your feeling and what is going on in the present moment.

● Pay attention to whatever you are doing. When you focus your mind on the tasks that you are set out to do, you will give it a sense of purpose and that helps to pay attention, undivided.

● Live in the present moment. We often get stuck in the past. Sometimes it is just painful experiences that we cannot shrug off. You need to realize that what has happened can't be changed. It has already happened so accept it and let go of it. The best way to avoid thinking of the past is by focusing back on the present moment. As Thich Nhat Hanh said, "People have a hard time letting go of their suffering. Out of fear of the unknown, they prefer suffering that is familiar."

● Do not get too caught up in the future. There is nothing wrong with planning for what is coming or the next moment, but don't let the fear of the unknown and the concerns about the next moment affect your present. Learn to live in the present moment. If you worry too much about the future, you will not be able to appreciate your present moment, which is happening right now.

● Sometimes it is okay to do nothing. Just spend some time alone in a quiet place and savor the environment just the way it is. Sitting quietly is the best way to empty your mind. Sitting meditation helps to enhance mindfulness. You can also perform various exercises while you meditate. Meditation is known to reduce stress, anxiety, and depression can reduce your chances of getting cancer.

● Don't get caught up in negative emotions. Let go of judgments. When you start focusing on your present moment, you may start observing a lot of things but you have not noticed before. While mindful observation is good, try not to judge what is going on around you. Embrace your emotions. Negative emotions will come and go. Being resilient and accept it. Let the positive and negative emotions pass. Detach. Don't drift into the past or the future. Remain in the present.

● Don't judge people around you for their actions, but empathize with their situation. When you don't try to predict how someone's behavior can affect the future, you will automatically stop judging. Don't let your past positive or negative emotions burden your present. If you don't let go off your past, you will keep comparing the positive moments of your past to your present. As Buddha said, "You can only lose what you cling to."

- Be compassionate towards others. When you practice mindfulness you will learn not to judge anyone. You will start to understand and sympathize with others. Don't expect others to share the same perspective as you. Empathize with your fellow human beings, even the ones caught up in negativity and experiencing difficulties in their life.

The journey to mindfulness is very personal. It is a process of letting go of one's past and future. It is about treating others well and focusing on the present and on the way it makes you feel in this moment of life.

Chapter 12: Using Meditation To Improve Self-Compassion

Since self-compassion is in our mind, one of the most logical ways to develop it is through meditation. Self-compassion can be unlocked and this is something that can be fast tracked if you will allocate it with time and enough dedication. There are different ways of meditating for the development of self-compassion. One way involves listening to a series of meditation sounds. Another one involves the help of a professional and is focused on postures and chants.

This chapter will focus on a meditation type that is easy to accomplish, requires only a minimal amount of time, and has that proven capability to immediately produce positive results. For this meditation, you need to set aside at least 15 minutes of your time daily. The steps are as follows:

Pick a posture or position that will allow relaxation and alertness at the same time. Lying down on your back or just sitting will be okay.

Do the mindful breathing technique. Observe nothing, but the process of inhaling and exhaling.

Put your hands over your heart and bring to memory a person or a living thing with which you felt genuine acceptance. It is important that the thoughts you will generate upon thinking of them include natural joy and happiness.

Put into thought the imperfect nature of the person or thing that you are thinking about. Put into the picture the possible vulnerabilities such as illnesses, pain, misfortune, and other related things.

Feel the presence of this person or thing to your heart and wish them well with chants of affirmations. Wish them wellness, safety, happiness, and comfortable living.

Add yourself to the wishes that you are making. Instead of saying, "May you be safe", say "May you and I be safe". Repeat these wishes or affirmations over and over until you feel the presence of openness, acceptance, and kindness over your whole being.

Put your attention on your body. Scan it with your mind from head to toe.

Make wishes or affirmations for yourself. This is similar to step number 5.

Once you have achieved the feeling of safety, direct your attention and wishes to those parts of the body which may have unpleasant feelings or conditions. Wish these parts positively.

Slowly bring back your awareness to the connection between your mind and body.

Feel your connection to others through a common energy and let this be the bridge for you to understand them and understand all of your being. Remain relaxed for a few minutes in complete silence.

The meditation process mentioned above is designed to take your attention away from the many distractions of life today and focus your thoughts on things that matter most for your purpose. Practice it daily and you will see a great improvement on the level of your self-compassion.

Chapter 13: Advanced Meditation

Step Seven
You begin these steps once you have your own experiences with your mindfulness. In step seven, you begin to take control of the mindfulness sessions. In the sense that you turn a one-way street into a two way street. Whatever you do, do not allow this two way street to transmit simultaneously while receiving, that will bring you back to chaos.

All this while in being mindful, you have been observing the natural cadence of your breath. Now you will do that, and then continue to change the cadence of your breath into something different. This is an experiment in self-study. By doing this, you will get to know yourself, and know the result differs for everyone.

When you get to stage seven and you have full appreciation for your breath, now begin to count the time it takes you to breathe in naturally and count the pause between the breaths. Then count the time it takes to exhale and the pause at the end of that. Keep a mental note of that. Do not stop to write it down.

Once you do that, begin to match the exhale times with the inhale times. So if you inhaled for 4 seconds, and exhaled for 5 second, slow down the inhalation to make it five-seconds as well. Match in and out consciously and practice that. That is the objective of step seven.

Step Eight

It will take some time to get to manage your breathing rates. More importantly, what you are teaching yourself to do is manage the two-way flow of communication. When you control your breathing, you are teaching your consciousness to communicate.

Once you get this, it's time to manage the pauses between the two strokes of breath. Measure the inhale-pause and compare it to the exhale-pause. Figure out which one you want to use and match one to the other. I will take some getting used to. You cannot force this, as you will end up feeling physically ill if you do. Forcing your breathing to much will make you hyperventilate. If there is too much difference between the intake stroke and the exhale-stroke, then change a little of both.

At the end of step eight, you will be able to balance your breathing consciously. Do not make this a habit. Habits are the opposite of mindfulness and thus not something you want to participate in if you want to advance your meditation.

Step Nine

The last eight steps have brought you from a state of chaos to the state of peace and a state of acceptance. This state that you now occupy is a conduit that is unblocked and able to transmit and receive across space and time. Everything is as it should be.

In step nine, you will now be able to add another dimension to your meditation. You will now be able to ask for answers to questions you may have about anything. The answers will come to you in the form of imaginations. Remember we talked about this in the first chapter. This is the second form of imagination - a higher form. It is the kind of imagination that Einstein was talking about.

Imaginations are not really imaginations. Imaginations are answers to questions we pose to our subconscious. The subconscious then returns an answer that it pucks from the infinite universe and presents it to us as answers.

In step nine, we will use meditation to enhance our questions and be open to their answers in our imagination.

Everything that we seek to know and understand is ours if we chose to ask for it and wait for the response. It is all within us and the first step to doing that is developing our ability to mediate with mindfulness.

The one thing you can consider as a bonus in this book, which is about meditation and mindfulness, is that you will now learn that when you refine your ability to be mindful and meditate, everything you could ever desire is yours.

Step Ten

Once you have learned how to do all this in isolation - in your dark and quiet room, you will need to do this everywhere else. It doesn't matter if you are an artist sitting in front of your easel, or a fighter pilot in his cockpit, mindfulness can be used by everyone in any situation. Always remain mindful of your exact place in space and time and do only that one thing in that one moment. When you practice this, you will find that your subconscious will step in and take care of the heavy lifting.

The one thing that you will need to learn to complete yourself, is that wherever you are and a distraction presents itself that causes your to fall out of mindfulness, just return to your breathing and you will be able to return to your state of peace.

Chapter 14: "A Series Of Breaths"

"One breath" is easy to migrate into two, then in three, then so on and so forth.

We can do as many of these "breaths" as we want. We have carefully folded out of them, like bricks, an excellent solid building of stable and level practice. Comparison with bricks is perhaps the most suitable since the quality of each individual element is important when building. The better our bricks, the stronger and safer the building.

"One breath" is the quintessence of meditation; without an understanding of this simple element, there is no practice at all. That is why "One breath" is given so much time. No matter how much we spend in meditation, a minute or an hour, or maybe a day, no matter what kind of meditation it is. "One breath" will be the basis of any practice. Having comprehended it, we will comprehend the essence of the process.

Our goal is to return to a forgotten and very unusual state for us, the here and now.
Obstacles to this meditation process?
The paradox of the work of our minds is that we do everything in order not to be in the present moment. More on this in the next chapter, now I just want to designate this as the main difficulty not only in the practice of meditation but also in life in general. The total lack of consciousness in the present moment has already become the subject of medical research. And the term "procrastination" is familiar to most of the inhabitants of the modern world. Returning to here and now, to the place where our life actually happens, is our task as part of the practice of meditation. "One breath" becomes our key to this, the first step. Having made it,

we ask ourselves a question: what does the second step look like?

If we have spent some time (several days or a week) practicing "One Breath," then we may want to try to do what is defined as:

Technique "Breath Series"
The series consists of several "One Breath" cycles. How many cycles to bring into the series is up to each of us to decide. You can start with two or three. Or you can start with five. The main thing is to focus on breathing.

You can close your eyes, sit down, or just stop where we are at the moment, and start. We count breathing, starting at the moment of inhalation and ending at the moment of exhalation. It is possible that the first time we can do up to ten cycles. This is more than enough. Maybe less. And this is also normal. You shouldn't do a lot at once. It's better to do another "Breath Series" a little bit later.

We can distribute the "Breath Series" by day as follows:
- immediately after waking up;
- before breakfast;
- in the car, before going to work, studying (in the hallway before going out, if there is no car, or at the home office if working at home);
- at work or at school at any convenient time;
- before lunch;
- after lunch at any convenient time;
- if there is a meeting, brainstorming or another group discussion at work in terms of the day, you can invite your colleagues to hold a "Breath Series" together (invite everyone to try to come to here and now to improve the process of discussing agenda issues as previously done with "One Breath");
- in the car, before going home, or also in the corridor/office before going out, if there is no car;

- before dinner (there is nothing wrong with not rushing to throw at food, but try to leave everything that is not related to food outside the plate. Otherwise we can start eating our worries, not food);
- before bedtime.

Of course, this may sound like something difficult to remember, but if we forget to make something from this list, it's okay if we made half great. Less is good. It's more elegant. Let's do more. The main thing is that we do not need to feel guilty, we are not obliged to anyone, we can simply not do it, and then do it, or not do it again. This is normal, after all. We spent so much time in an unconscious state, which makes it very difficult to enter the conscious phase in one day.

The main rule in meditation is not right and wrong. We either do or do not.

However, it is important to do.

The Breath Series is a new stage in our practice. One "Series" takes about a minute. Maybe even less. Is it difficult to find a minute for something simple, quiet, and relaxing? It's hard not to find this minute; that's what makes this approach unique.

At the height of the working day, in the middle of working on a complex report or presentation, preparing for a meeting, and maybe sitting at home, during a break between a series of your favorite TV series or news releases, between checking "what's new on Facebook," between shouts to children or parents, or in a car in a traffic jam, at a traffic light, before a railway crossing, after talking with a traffic police officer and before setting off again.

Give yourself and your mind, which is needed, needed fresh, alive, active less than one minute. Why put off? You can do it right now. The past has already disappeared, the future does not yet exist, all that we have is the present moment. Can we afford to let it go? Lose the only thing that is real?

And the last - these techniques are very simple, but this is exactly what we need at the initial stage. They give us a clear idea of what needs to be done, without clogging the mind with the difficult and incomprehensible. A discouraging the desire to move on in practice.

Chapter 15: Mindfulness At Home

There is perhaps no easier place to practice mindfulness than in your own home as it is there that you have the greatest level of control over yourself and your surroundings. In fact, once you get in the habit of practicing mindfulness on a regular basis there will hardly be anything that you can do that won't lend itself to practicing mindfulness with nothing more than a little extra thought and a little more practice. Who knows, the ways you can practice mindfulness in the home may even surprise you.

Practice mindfulness while taking care of everyday chores

Prior to beginning your journey to understand mindfulness meditation you likely considered taking care of your household chores to be the epitome of drudgery and menial labor. Once you look at them through the lens of mindfulness meditation, however you will soon find that they are one of the best opportunities to practice mindfulness meditation while still being outwardly productive to boot. Remember, any activity that has a physical component that doesn't require your full and active attention can easily become an outlet for mindfulness meditation as long as you approach it in the right way.

When it is time to tackle your chores, the first thing that you are going to want to do is to take a few moments before hand to clear your mind and get in touch with the signals that your body is sending you. With your mind primed, dive into the moment to moment nature of the activity you are pursuing with the goal of limiting thought to the extreme. Instead, consider the way your hands feel as they go through the motions of whatever it is you are doing. Consider the information your eyes are providing you as the task alters the physical world in one way or another as well as the smells that accompany the task and what it is that they signify. Finally, once you are completed take another moment to enjoy the feeling of accomplish that is sure to manifest from a job well done and consider the difference of the before and after nature of the task you just completed. For the best results, prepare everything you need to do for several chores beforehand so that you can string the periods of mindfulness together as much as possible. With practice, you can easily create a state of mindfulness that lasts for an hour, if not more.

Practice mindfulness while you are bathing
It doesn't matter if your bathing habits skew towards the morning or the evening, you can easily use this time to practice mindfulness meditation and either help you get ready to start your day off right or to further decompress when the day is at an end. While most people rush through their daily bath or shower with nary a thought, this period of time is rife with sensations for your body to track while at

the same time being devoid of any of the distractions that might plague your mindfulness meditation in other settings.

Before you begin your bathing ritual take an extra moment to center yourself and get in touch with your body. If it is early in the morning make an effort to put off all thoughts of the day ahead and if it is evening push out everything that has happened during the day in an effort to get into the moment as quickly as possible. Once you are ready, start by considering the feel of the water on your skin and how the hot, or cold, water feels engulfing your body completely and running down your skin.

Use the repetitive tasks that you are performing as a gateway to reach a mental state that is free of anything but the sensations you are feeling right now. Smell is also an extremely powerful sense in this instance and focusing on the scents that surround you is also a fantastic way to push out other thoughts as they try to intrude.

Practice mindfulness while exercising

While it might seem surprising, the mindset of the average individual who is exercising is already remarkably similar to the mindset of someone who is practicing mindfulness meditation. This is caused by the fact that exercise automatically pushes the sensations that the body is sending out to the forefront of the mind and the concentration that many types of exercise require in order to see the best results. As such, it then only takes a little push to tip this type of mindset over into mindfulness meditation in its entirety. As an added bonus studies show that those who practice mindfulness while they exercise are known to report an increase in their level of endurance as well as a measurable boost to their overall performance.

The key to pushing the one into the other is to reduce your focus on getting everything you are doing exactly right and to instead focus on the body parts that you are pushing to their limits, how they feel as they move and the sensations they are providing you with as you put them through their paces. Each time you complete an exercise and move onto the next you can use the pause in the forward momentum as an opportunity to refocus your attention on the moment and banish any stray thoughts that may have crept in while your focus was elsewhere.

While you are focusing on the moment it is important to not lose track of what you are doing entirely as you may push yourself too hard and accidentally cause undue strain on your body. With that in mind, it doesn't matter what type of exercise you enjoy or where you perform it, there are likely going to be a whole host of sights, sounds and smells to draw you into the moment as thoroughly as possible. For the best results, start off with a focus on what it is you are doing and let yourself get into a rhythm. From there, let your body take care of itself and use the sensations the exercise provides to push everything else out of your mind so that you can find the sense of inner peace that you are striving for.

Practice being mindful while utilizing social media

Despite the fact that it might seem counterintuitive, if you make a concentrated effort to do so, you can even practice mindfulness meditation while you are utilizing social media of all types. While the siren's call of a social media notification can easily draw you out of the moment during several types of mindfulness meditation, if you allocate a set time with which to check up on what your friends are doing you can actually find a state of mindfulness while doing so.

For this type of mindfulness meditation to work, the first thing that you are going to want to do is to eliminate any other potential distractions before you get to work. This is an extremely crucial step due to the fact that a majority of people check social media sites as a means of multitasking. With any distractions out of the way, you will first want to clear your mind and make an effort to inhabit the moment as much as possible. With the proper mindset obtained you can then look at the pictures or text that relates to your personal history with an eye towards inhabiting those past moments as thoroughly as possible.

For every picture that you see or tweet that you read consider what was taking place at its time of inception. Remember the way you felt at the time and let the memory wash over you completely. Make an effort to put yourself into the time and place in question by remembering the various signals that your body was providing you with at the time. Once you have this in mind, you will then want to go even deeper into the memory by starting with the smells you can remember. If the day was hot or cold, try and conjure up the way the temperature felt on your skin and if it was loud, consider what it is your ears were taking in. With enough practice, you will find that you are able to block out all external stimuli and exist solely in a previous moment.

Practice reflecting on the preceding day in a mindful fashion

Prior to going to bed at the end of the day you may find it helpful to practice mindfulness meditation, especially if you have difficulty falling asleep or staying asleep due to stresses that come up naturally during the day. This process of offloading your stress from the day can be done either by taking a mental inventory, but you may find the process more beneficial if you instead write down what has been troubling you.

As usual, you will want to begin by taking a few moments to center yourself and to work to get into the type of mindset that will make it easier to find a state of mindfulness once you get into the bulk of the exercise. When you get ready to write down what you remember about your day you may find it helpful to write out by hand what you remember rather than typing up a journal as the tactile experience of writing can be an easy way to tie yourself to the moment. Likewise, when you want to go back and read what you have previously written you will have that tactile experience of writing it the first time to reflect on in addition to focusing on what happen in the entry that you are reading.

When you start writing it is important that you take stock of the day as a whole and make an effort to include absolutely everything that happened to you in the past twenty-four hours, regardless of how meaningless it seems at the time. As you write you are going to want to commit yourself to remembering each moment as fully as possible, complete with all of the various stimuli that were taking place as the memory was made. With practice, this detailed examination of your day will make it easier for you to pick out various sensations that you might have missed while practicing other forms of mindfulness meditation.

Once you have a little bit more perspective on the events that have unfolded and read back through what you have written you will often find that the individual moments that seem the most innocuous have the greatest impact on the future. Once you have written enough journal entries to begin to notice this type of pattern you will then be primed to notice all of the little moments more throughout your day and let moments of mindfulness slip in as well.

Practice mindfulness meditation to start your day out right

No matter how rushed you feel you are in the morning, you can find a few minutes to practice mindfulness meditation if you make a concentrated effort to do so. The easiest way to do so is by taking a few extra moments to really savor your favorite morning drink be it coffee, tea or even soda or an energy drink. What's more, if you shower in the mornings as well, you can string together a group of mindfulness meditation sessions practically from the moment you wake up until you reach your workplace. From there, if you do it right you can be mindful throughout your day right up until it is time for bed.

The morning mindfulness meditation session is one of the easiest to get the hang of as the first cup of an energizing beverage of the day is naturally more potent than those that follow it as your body has had all the hours you were asleep to get the caffeine out of your system ensuring that the first jolt is the most powerful that you are going to feel throughout the day. This, in turn, naturally draws you into the present more fully, especially if you take the extra time to really appreciate it. Remember, this may be the only truly relaxing moment of your entire day, it is best to make it count.

For the best results, you are going to want to wake up with the idea of mindfulness on the brain. As you wake in the morning take a few extra moments to consider the thoughts that are already racing through your head and consider why they are there without interacting with them directly. If your thoughts are all about the day ahead, make a concentrated effort to push them aside until you have successfully finished your morning mindfulness meditation routine. If possible, go ahead and slip into a state of mindfulness directly after taking stock of your mental inventory.

Once you are properly adapted to the moment the next thing that you are going to want to do is to pay special attention to the preparation of your drink of choice. While there is certainly going to be more to be aware of if you are grinding coffee beans and filling an espresso machine, even pulling out a teabag or taking a cold drink from the refrigerator has plenty of sensations to offer when it comes to locking you in place in the moment. As you go through the routine of preparation consider the anticipation of what is to come, the smell of the beverage brewing or the feel of the cold can against your skin. Regardless of your drink of choice it is important to really savor the moments before you take your first sip and take in the world around you as much as possible. The goal here is to be able to completely recall the events leading up to your first drink if you are planning to write about it at the end of the day.

Once you are ready to actually take your first drink, you want to find a quiet spot to sit and really appreciate the first sip. Take in the smell of the drink, the smell of it and the feel as it hits your tongue and rolls down your throat. Focus on the feel of the cup or can in your hand and the heat or the cold that is radiating from it. Try and remain in the moment as much as possible and chart the course of the caffeine as it invigorates every part of your body one by one. As you feel the liquid running through your body consider the benefits it is providing you and how it is giving you the energy to face the coming day head on.

During this period, it is important to give the beverage the full sum of your attention, if you find your mind wandering the details of the day simply refocus and bring your mind back to the task at hand. Once you are finished, take note of the way the empty vessel feels now that it is devoid of the precious liquid. Finally, take another few moments to take in the silence around you before readying yourself to start your day in earnest.

Practice dancing or listening to music mindfully

It doesn't matter who you are dancing with or why you are dancing in the first place, dancing itself is an inherently mindful act. Proper dancing requires the complete focus of the dancer both to ensure that the body follows as it should but also of the music, the tempo and the way they work together to affect the body. If you already love to dance, then all you need to do is be aware of the ways in which it helps you be mindful to take full advantage of their effects.

Much like dancing, playing music in such a way that it demands your attention is an inherently mindful action. As long as you take the time to focus on the moment and consider the way your body relates to the creation of each individual note. Consider the other musicians you are playing with and the ways the smallest change in what you are doing can affect the flow of the whole. For those who are not musically inclined, chanting may be a viable alternative. Repeating a phrase or mantra can be an effective way of achieving a higher state of mindfulness. Like with dancing, an understanding of the mindful principles at play will make you more aware of them in the moment.

Practice being mindful with your family

While oftentimes practicing mindfulness meditation means spending time alone, this isn't a prerequisite for practicing successfully. In fact, practicing mindfulness meditation with your family is actually a great way to spend time with your loved ones, as long as you do it properly that is. The best way to go about doing so is to use group meal times to foster a sense of mindfulness with everyone involved. While it might seem difficult to get multiple people to focus on the moment, as long as things are handled properly, and all technology is left outside the kitchen and/or dining room then the process is easier than you might expect.

First things first, you are going to want to get everyone involved in the preparation for the food, you don't need to make a big deal about the mindfulness aspects inherent in the process, all you need to do is simply encourage everyone to give their full attention to their assigned preparation task. Once everyone has settled into the rhythm of food preparation then you will all be on your way to focusing on the moment to the exclusion of all else.

Once the food is prepared, gather everyone around the table and, before anyone takes their first bite, take a few moments to start your deep breathing exercises and consider all of the sensations that the fresh meal is sending to your body. The first few times you try this with your family you will want to point out the sights of the meal that you have prepared as well as the smells that are wafting out from it. Eventually, this will become simply another part of the meal and you won't have to break your own state of mindfulness to ensure that everyone else is following along.

In addition to taking in the preliminary sights and smells of the meal you will want to make eye contact with each member of your family and as you do so contemplate the special connection that you both share thanks to the meal you have helped prepare together and encourage family members to do the same with everyone else. Finally, you will want to audibly express your gratitude that you can all be together right here, right now, in this particular moment in time.

With the preliminary mindfulness meditation out of the way, it will then be time to get to the main event, the consumption of the meal that you have all come together to prepare for one another. Prior to starting you will want to make a point of cautioning your family to avoid eating to rapidly and to instead make an effort to really taste each bite of food you take, and enjoy the sensations it provides.

As you eat you will want to anchor yourself to the moment by considering all of the flavors that the food provides, feel your teeth tear into it and break it down and feel any spices that may be used as they create a physical sensation in your mouth. You will want to picture each bite as it moves into your stomach and consider the various vitamins and nutrients that it is passing on to your body. If you try hard enough, you should be able to taste the whole of the universe in every bite. Focus on this thought as you eat and consider the joy you feel when receiving the bounty of the universe and sharing it with the people you love. Breaking bread with someone forms a unique bond with that person quite unlike anything else, consider this as you eat and focus on the moment to ensure it lasts as long as possible.

Another good thing about making a habit out of eating mindfully is that it will naturally draw you to meal options that are naturally healthier overall as processed foods that are full of artificial preservatives don't typically require enough preparation to draw in the entire family. Not only will a careful consideration of the food you eat lead you to feel full more quickly than you otherwise will, such a careful consideration of the food will also often make the meal taste more delicious than those meals which are consumed quickly and without a second thought. As you get more in touch with what you are eating you will also find that it is much easier to determine if you are really in need of sustenance or if you are considering eating for some other, less healthy, alternative.

One downside of practicing mindfulness meditation with the entire family is that if one or more members aren't on board, the exercise loses much of its potency. As such, you are going to want to take special care to ensure that everyone is on the same page for the best results. In order to do this, you may want to start by explaining that the food that you are about to eat is a direct gift from the universe at large. By explaining every step that was required for the food to get from where it was created all the way to your table you will add a weight to the meal that is often lost when people are disproportionately disassociated from their food as most people are in this day and age.

While the preparation of the meal and the first few minutes once you all sit down to eat should be relatively quiet, that doesn't mean that the entire meal should be consumed in silence. If this were the case then you would be little better off than eating alone. You will, however, want to make it a point to keep conversation focused on the meal itself. To get the ball rolling you are going to want to foster conversation about the quality of the meal, its nutritional value and the general bounty of what has been provided for you. While you won't always be able to keep the conversation in this sphere, you will want to make a point of avoiding any negative conversation or heated debates as these types of topics will only make it more difficult for everyone to remain mindful throughout the meal.

While eating mindfully will likely make each meal seem as though it lasts longer than you are used to, the reality of the situation is that a mindful meal should last no longer, or be any larger, than a normal meal and may actually even be smaller than the meals that you were eating before as your greater level of concentration will often allow you to eat smaller meals while feeling just as full as you otherwise would.

Chapter 16: Mindfulness Meditation For Deep Relaxation

If you try to imagine what deep relaxation feels like, you will realize that it makes you feel like you are floating in the clouds, open, limitless and carefree. You will be utterly immersed in the present moment, so much so that your mind is filled only with contentment, kindness and gratitude. In today's fast-paced world, you may think that deep relaxation is unachievable, but the truth is that mindfulness meditation can help you get there.

Reduce Stress

Before you begin your meditation session for deep relaxation, however, you must first understand that relaxation is only achievable when you are not in a state of stress. As you may know, stress is experienced when the mind perceives something as a threat, whether it is from external forces (such as your boss criticizing you) or internal (such as a humiliating memory from the past).

It will be difficult for you to get into a state of deep relaxation when your mind is completely stressed out. The first thing you should do is to become more mindful of how stressed you feel. It may sound counterintuitive to do so, but when you acknowledge your feelings of stress, your mind can deal with the issue directly. The sooner it does, the sooner you can reduce your stress levels.

Here are some of the steps you can apply when practicing mindfulness to help lower your stress levels (especially prior to meditating for deep relaxation):

Step 1: Go to a quiet, relaxing place where no one will disturb you for a while. Sit or lie down comfortably.

Step 2: Relax your eyelids and place your hands on your knees or lap if you are sitting, or on your belly if you are lying down.

Step 3: Bring your awareness to your breathing. Are you breathing naturally, or are you taking short gasps? Describe how you are breathing.

Example: I've have only just noticed that I have been holding my breath. I am now taking in short breaths.

Step 4: Shift your awareness towards your heart. Describe how fast your heart is beating. On a scale of 1 to 10, with ten being really fast, how fast is your heartbeat?

Example: My heart is beating so fast, I'd say it is a 10.

Step 5: Shift your awareness towards your mind. You are an observer of your own thoughts. Notice the thoughts that cross your mind without judgment. What do your thoughts tell you? Can you tell what has been plaguing your thoughts?

Example: My thoughts are about the exam tomorrow. My thoughts are full of worry that I might fail in the exam. My thoughts are about me not concentrating well enough while studying.

Step 6: Describe the thoughts in relation to your emotions. What are those thoughts that cause you to feel stressed? What kinds of emotions are evoked because of those thoughts?

Example: My worrisome thoughts are making me feel anxious and stressed. My negative thoughts are making me feel depressed and panicky.

Step 7: Shift your awareness to your current reactions to the thoughts. Ask yourself whether your current reactions are helpful to your stressful situation or not. Take your time, especially if the stressful thoughts are overwhelming.

Example: My worrisome thoughts are making me feel stressed. Is this helpful to me? Will I be able to do well in the exam because of this? I feel that this is not helpful.

Step 8: Acknowledge your situation then mindfully respond to your current reactions based on the conclusion you have drawn. Become mindful of the present moment and how you have the power to choose how to use it.

Example: I feel stressed out because of the exam tomorrow. I cannot focus on my studies because of this. My mind is a jumble right now. I need to relax.

Once you have become mindful of the cause of your stress, you will find that it is easier to relax. After this, you may choose to write down any solutions you may have come up with during the session. You can then proceed to doing mindful meditation for deep relaxation.

Mindfulness Meditation for Deep Relaxation

Meditating for deep relaxation will help calm your emotions and thoughts and enable you to see things more clearly. You can then face your problems with a fresh and positive perspective. Even if do not have any issues in your life right now, it would still do your mind and body a lot of good to relax deeply and have the tools to deal with life's difficulties which will surely come at some point.

The following steps will guide you through a mindful deep relaxation practice. Take your time to practice this without falling asleep. After the session, notice how refreshed and invigorated you feel.

Step 1: Find a quiet place where you can lie down or sit back comfortably. Turn on some relaxing meditation music, if you want. For instance, try searching for "Deep Healing Tibetan Music" online and play it.

Step 2: Lie down on a comfortable mattress or armchair. Keep your back straight, and your shoulders relaxed. Allow your eyelids to droop or close. Breathe naturally.

Step 3: Place one hand on your belly and another on your chest.

Step 4: Take at least 10 deep breaths with your mind focusing entirely on each breath. Notice how your belly rises with each inhale, and falls with each exhale.

Observe how the hand on your chest remains still.

Step 5: Continue to breathe in and out deeply until you notice a change in your heart rate and breathing.

Step 6: Shift your awareness towards your heart. Is it a steady beat? If it continues to beat fast, shift your focus back towards your breathing and continue to take deep breaths.

Do not criticize your heart for continuing to beat fast. Simply focus on each deep breath until you feel lighter and more relaxed.

When your mind starts to drift towards other thoughts, observe the thoughts as if you are an outsider looking in then draw your mind back towards your deep breaths.

Step 7: Shift your focus towards the relaxing music. Notice the rise and fall of the melody without judgment. Let the vibrations from the song resonate into your ear then expand throughout your body. Fill your mind completely with the sound.

Step 8: Shift your awareness towards your heart. Feel it beating steadily inside your chest. Breathe in deeply as you focus on your heart. Breathe out slowly. Continue to focus on your heart with each breath until you feel your entire body become completely relaxed.

Step 9: Become aware of the feeling of relaxation. In your mind's eye, scan your body for any tense parts, and then allow each part, one by one, to relax and sink into the mattress or chair.

For example, if you become aware that your hands are clenched, allow them to relax with each breath. Do not make any judgments of any tension you have. Simply allow that part of your body to release the tension when it is ready.

Step 10: Focus your awareness towards your entire body. Notice how completely relaxed it is now that each part of it has willingly surrendered itself.

Step 11: Shift your awareness back to your breath. This time, do not try to control it. Allow your body to breathe as it naturally would.

If your mind starts to linger to your thoughts other than each breath, gently draw it back. Immerse yourself completely to observing each inhale and exhale.

Step 12: At this point, you may already be in the state of deep relaxation. Stay aware of the complete comfort you are feeling in this present moment. You may come out of the meditation when you are ready to face the rest of your day.

After achieving deep relaxation, you will notice that your mind will become clearer and more positive. You will begin to see life from a different perspective and see the bigger picture.

If your mind starts to drift to sleep, avoid fighting it. Sleep is but a natural response to help your mind rest and rejuvenate. Of course, if you think you still have some things to do after the session, then it would be a good idea to set an alarm with a gentle tone, so you can prevent yourself from falling asleep as you settle into deep relaxation.

Chapter 17: Commit To A Regular Practice That Feels Natural

How often should you practice?

Ideally, we are always in the present. But our alarms eventually get the best of us. That's why certain times of the day are best to build a practice before you need it in crisis or under pressure.

Waking up is not only the first moment to be mindful, it happens every day. If you're not a morning person, after your first cup of coffee might be better, but what we know each day is that there is time before 'the list' kicks in. Your alarm wants problems solved and the list checked off. If you start the morning off with pilates, yoga, sitting and reading the paper slowly, making coffee like a monk, or just watching the sun rise, your brain starts the day fully functioning. Service men and women rotate looking for bombs in the hot seat of a Humvee or crewing the turret of a tank because their brains can only focus intently for ninety minutes or less. One of the ways to fight cognitive fatigue in your day is to make sure your brain isn't spinning first thing.

Meals may be the most obvious time to be mindful. Instead of wolfing down your food, even if you only have a few minutes, slow your chewing. French culture demands slow, intentional eating because food is a gift and the meal is sacred time. Too many of us miss the opportunity to turn down our alarms every time we eat. Even a candy at your desk can become a mindful practice. Enjoy its flavor for five, six, even seven minutes before it melts away.

Closing time could be the most undervalued chance to be mindful in the world today. It's no longer just Western culture that is driving twenty-four seven. 'It's five o'clock somewhere' is a not just a mantra to inspire libation, it is also a reminder that at some place right now people have stopped doing and started being. They are relaxing with each other. They are loving each other. At the end of the day, shut down the machines. The device in your pocket dinging stops the being if it triggers your alarm. Instead, have an end to your work day where you truly make downtime a priority.

The rule of thumb we all need to follow in building a mindful practice is **transitions and 12**. If every time you transition from one part of your day to the next — leaving the house or office, getting into and out of the car, between meetings or appointments, at each stop as you chauffeur your children from one activity to the next — you do an exercise, your brain will transform. Traffic won't bother you (or at least not as much). The worthless meeting might suddenly be valuable or you have the gumption to wrap it up quicker. You will enjoy the ups and downs of your day because you make space to be rather than react.

And each of us, as Dr. Jha discovered, need 12 minutes of scheduled being. 12 straight minutes may feel like a lot at first, but it will become a tiny gift to yourself each day. That meditation time is not optional for optimal brain health. How you meditate is. You can sit, breathe, walk, look, listen, concentrate, imagine, chant, or simply 'be.' What you can't do is have a day without it. The habit of meditating each day creates deeper and deeper awareness that nothing is more important than being in this moment.

Each of these suggestions has a simple hope: consistency. Going to yoga a few times a week is amazing in so many ways. It proves to your brain that you can turn down the alarm and be present. But it simply won't be enough to overcome the stressors of modern life. What we all need is regular daily and hourly exercises that become our habit and ultimately who we are.

Chapter 18: How To Know What You Want And Go After It

In the last couple of chapters, we've focused on using CBT to reduce stress. And we've seen how this can indirectly lead to advancements in your career thanks to things like the law of attraction.

But what about motivating yourself toward something? What if you're not frozen by fear and stress but simply by tiredness and indifference? What if you don't know what it is you want out of life, or how to structure a goal so that you can get there? You can't very well work toward what you want when you don't know what that is!

Vision, Not Goal

The first thing we're going to do is to introduce just a very subtle shift in the way you approach these ideas. And specifically, this will mean having a vision and not a goal.

What is the difference between a vision and a goal? A vision is much more abstract but at the same time, more tangible.

A goal is to lose 1 stone in 10 weeks. A vision is to be the same you, but fitter, healthier and more attractive – running outdoors with a healthy looking tan and waking up every morning with tons of energy to get up and at-tack the day.

Which of those things is more motivating? For most people, the answer will be the vision.

The other great thing about visions is that most of us already have them, even if we don't know it. If I ask you what your goal in life is, then you might not be able to answer. But if I ask you to just imagine your perfect life, then you might find it easier to do. Perhaps you're sitting on a beautiful beach somewhere? Perhaps you're living in a massive mansion? Maybe you're rich in a skyscraper somewhere?

If you're still struggling to come up with a vision that you can work toward, then some other questions to ask are things like: who are your role models (and what do they have in common)? When was the last time you were truly happy? What did you want to be when you were a kid?

It doesn't have to be super concrete – wanting to be rich, wanting more time with your family or wishing you weren't at work is fine! And if you do have something really concrete – wishing you were a famous rock star – then that's fine too.

From here, the next thing to do is to take that vision and break it down into steps. This is another important point and it's once again something that a lot of people get wrong. If you are working toward a goal rather than a vision, then you might, as per our previous example, be working toward losing X amount of weight in N amount of time.

This is a fine aim but it's far too distant and too outside your control to be useful. When it comes to the crunch and you need to force yourself out the door to exercise, it's all too easy to just tell yourself you'll catch up on what you've missed later. You end up putting it off or making excuses and by the time that amount of time has passed and you haven't achieved what you were hoping, you just feel disappointed, disheartened and possibly depressed. Eventually, this leads to you giving up entirely!

So instead, we make steps toward our vision. This means coming up with a plan first and often you'll find it's easier than you think to accomplish the impossible – it just requires a bit of creative thought. For example, if you want to be a rock star you might take a less obvious route such as creating your own YouTube channel and posting your music regularly. If you build up a big enough following and you have enough obvious skill, then eventually this is highly likely to lead to an offer for a recording contract!

In other scenarios it might be a very easy set of steps – in order to lose weight, you might eat no more than 1800 calories every day and workout five times a week for 30 minutes. If you want to write a best selling novel, your goal might be to wake up one hour early and write for 40 minutes before work.

These are now incredibly simple steps that are highly within your control. You either fail or pass but it's entirely down to you. And if you do fail? You can simply try again the next day. Each day is a fresh challenge and there is no putting things off. Ultimately, this makes a goal much easier to stick to

– especially if you use the chain technique a lot of people use: creating a string of X's in a calendar so that you will find yourself not wanting to break the sequence by missing a workout or writing session!

This will seem detached from the goal at times but if the steps are good, then taking them every single day, week or month on a consistent basis will mean you're getting gradually closer to your aim.

Now all that's left is to motivate yourself and to get yourself in a mind set where you're willing to put in the time and work to get to where you want to be. How do you get yourself to get out of bed to go for a run at 5am when it's pouring with rain outside?

The answer is that you need to use a slightly altered form of CBT by focusing on the emotional reasons behind what you're doing. In other words, you need to think about the vision and you need to feel the vision. This is what will give you the release of the correct neurotransmitters to have the motivation to do it. You can also focus on what it is you're trying to avoid.

So if you're thinking about running in the morning and you can't find the willpower to do it, the answer is just to make the connection in your mind so that you link that step to the outcome you want. Visualize that version of yourself who is fit, healthy and ripped and picture yourself running in the sun during the summer.

Think about how it feels to never have this low energy and think about the alternative – getting gradually less and less fit and feeling gradually worse and worse with nothing that you can do to fix it.

And if you try this a few mornings and you find it doesn't work, then another consideration is to try setting yourself up some kind of video or script that you can read or watch when you wake up to do that for you. Feel the emotion, know that the step you're considering is what can get you there and then take the next step!

Chapter 19: What Is Mindfulness?

You may have come across the concept of mindfulness at some point in your life, but what is it exactly? The term originates from a translation of a Pali-term known as Sati. Sati is an element of Buddhist traditions. In recent popularity in the West. Sati was initiated by a man named Job Kabat-Zinn. Kabat-Zinn is a famous mindfulness meditation teacher and was the founder of a program known as Mindfulness-Based Stress Reduction at the medical center at the University of Massachusetts. We will be learning more about this in a later chapter.

So, what is mindfulness exactly? Some say that it is a psychological process where a person can bring their attention to both internal and external experiences to their mind at the present moment. For most people, they do this through the practice of meditation or yoga. Later in the chapters, will be discussing how you can bring these practices into your daily life. For now, it is important to understand the concept of mindfulness and how it is important for your health.

For some people, accepting what they are feeling is the most difficult concept for them. Unfortunately, this can become a pattern in their day to day life. From first falling into an initial bad experience, then feeling bad about what happens, which leads to feeling bad about feeling bad about a certain situation. As you can tell, this can become a vicious cycle and even worse, be detrimental to one's health! This is where mindfulness comes into play. If you are aware of your thoughts and feelings, you can break the cycle and learn to have a healthier thought process.

You may be thinking, "Well, accepting my feelings just isn't enough." While this may be true, it is certainly an amazing start. By accepting your thoughts, you can accept your feelings. By accepting your feelings, you can step back and take a good hard look at the situation. You can tell yourself that while what you are experiencing may not be ideal, it doesn't mean that you have to be defined by your stress. Instead, mindfulness will teach you that there are healthy ways to accept your thoughts and move on from the moment.

So, where do you begin with mindfulness? Some people have stated that it helps them to locate the emotion within their body. The first step is to realize that the emotion you are feeling is smaller than you are. This way, if you are bigger than the emotion, it means that the stress you are feeling is not everything that you are. By doing this, you can create a space between you as a person and the emotion that you are feeling. By creating space, you may feel like you aren't being suffocated by the problem.

How do you do this? How can you make a stress feeling small? Some have decided to locate the feeling of stress and personify it. For example, try asking yourself some of the following questions: What color is the stress? Does it have a certain texture? Perhaps your feeling is jagged or slimy. Does your stress have a shape? Does it change over a certain amount of time? By giving your stress character, it becomes separate from yourself, therefore, giving you a better grip on the reality of the stress.

According to Kabat-Zinn, his definition of mindfulness is, "…means paying attention in a particular way; on purpose, in the present moment, and nonjudgmentally." His definition highlights the fact that while you practice mindfulness, you must be accepting and always avoid harsh judgments. This gives you the ability to be aware of the experiences surrounding you without pushing the emotions away or even holding them inside. By accepting your emotions, you can be free of them.

While mindfulness involves conscious direction, it important to understand that "mindfulness" and "awareness" are not interchangeable terms. To be mindful, you have to be habitually aware of your feelings. One does not equal the other. If you are aware of a feeling, this does not necessarily mean that you are mindful. Instead, you have to be aware of the situation and then become mindful of it to accept the emotion that you are feeling.

Research studies have found that by being mindful, a large amount of the population have a positive correlation with having a better well-being as well as better health. Mindfulness is also effective to reduce rumination and worry, which have been known to contribute to illnesses such as depression and anxiety. This may be why mindfulness is practiced in psychology to help alleviate both mental and physical conditions of patients. By reducing patients stress through mindfulness, it has been known to help with both anxiety and drug addiction.

For most of us, we are only slightly aware of our thoughts. With this habit, it allows our negative emotions to wander in a very unrestricted way. By having no conscious to bring attention back to the emotion, there is no purpose to the negative emotion we are feeling. This is why we are taught mindfulness to have a purpose to our experiences. By being mindful, you can shape your mind and make your thoughts healthier. You may be asking yourself, what kind of situation would I use this in? For one example, we will be discussing some people's issues with food and the guilty conscious of eating and overeating.

In a health and diet conscious world, some of you may develop an extremely unhealthy relationship with food. While some of us are conscious of what we are putting into our bodies, other may not be. How can we become mindful of our relationship with food? By focusing on our thoughts while we are eating! When an individual is conscious of the process of eating, they can normally notice the sensation of eating such as flavor, color, texture, scent, and more. But, what happens when we are not mindful of what we are eating? Perhaps we are watching the television, talking with friends, reading the newspaper, or simply just thinking about other things. As your mind wanders, you may be not aware of what you are putting into your mouth or how much you are putting into your system. If you are barely aware of the physical sensation of eating, you are probably even less aware of your thoughts and emotions.

Life can be simple, happy, complicated or sad. Life itself is unpredictable, and change is an inevitable factor that goes along with it. Change can hit us in the hardest way possible and leave us on our knees or stumble down. With it, we may seem to lose contact to our inner self and forget the things that make us who we are. When troubles come along the way, we tend to get caught up in the tempest of our emotions and points of view. Ultimately, as we continue our battle to survive, little by little, a piece of us seems to drift astray from what or who we were supposed to be. Until one day, we sit on one corner and feel as if we're lost in the depth of our own thoughts thinking of what ifs in life, re-evaluating our goals and what we have achieved so far. It's fun to say that the bulb of our vivid imagination is always at work and it's doing its trick on our preoccupied selves, turning our frets into a technicolor visions of the future — however, it doesn't work that way. In the end, we have to face reality as it is and deal with the challenges that sprout from anywhere. We have to admit that somehow we failed ourselves, not just in terms of achievements in life but the mere fact that we have deprived ourselves of a healthy or happy way of living.

How can I say so? I've undergone quarter-life crisis and the struggle is definitely real. It even came to a point when I can't even manage to pull myself together and can't even be productive enough at work. Instead, I was unaware that I was already dragging a load of negativity as I continue to sulk. I tried to convince myself that it's ok but my heart says otherwise. Honestly, I can't even think clearly because my thoughts are in complete disarray. It's like I'm trapped in a war within me. Just like what Robert Louis Stevenson wrote in The Strange Case of Dr. Jekyll and Mr. Hyde, "In each of us, two natures are at war – the good and the evil. All our lives the fight goes on between them and one of them must conquer. But in our own hands lies the power to choose – what we want most to be we are." Truly, each one of us has our own chaos within us, but certainly, we have to combat the evil and let the good prevail. Evil comes in different forms and one of which is negativity – a power so cruel that it sucks up all the good and leave you with misery. It was the worst feeling ever. Only you and I have the supremacy over it, and the key is to make the right choice, and I made mine before of which I didn't have any regret. Yes, we had our bad days, but I realized that it's never an excuse to lead a miserable life.

Buddha once said, "Do not dwell in the past, do not dream of the future, concentrate the mind on the present moment." It implies that we should forgive ourselves, accept our once defeat at the shot of life, leave the past behind and just learn from it in order for us to take another chance of moving forward to be better. Just like butterflies, we can allow ourselves to morph beautifully and reveal our true colors. But first, it is important that we find our true inner self.

Though it may be easier to blame or point the finger at something or someone that may have caused the disappointments, in as much as it's harder to accept the truth and move on, still doing the latter breaks the chains that bind us from the haunting experiences of the past. We have to find that path which will aid us in restoring our self-adoration that once was lost when we were dumbfounded by our failures and mistakes. All we have to do is feel the determination deep within us - a strong will to let go of what hurts us or leaves us melancholy and take a leap of faith towards the bright tomorrow that awaits us. The only person standing between you and your dream is you, and the main element that keeps you from doing what you have to do is FEAR. One way or another you have to conquer it even if it may be tough – just remind yourself that you're as powerful as you think so don't let it take control.

I had my share of less fortunate chapters in my life, and I know you have your own too. I have my fears, but I learned to triumph over it, and then I knew that I'm the only one who could do it; not anyone or anybody else. I found myself better than I was yesterday and all that changed when I made a choice – to be Mindful. I believe that one you could achieve it too! Remember, just will it and it will be yours. You have to stand guard by your goals in rediscovering your true purpose and existence in this world. You may be wondering, how to be mindful? What does being mindful truly mean?

Mindfulness can be described in four simple words: Living in the Moment. It's the condition of appreciating the present situation or moments and living it as it is without having to worry about the past or the distant future. You have to pay attention to what's happening now while you keep your mind rejuvenated to embrace the full experience of the present moments. It is the state of being where your thoughts don't wander off into possibilities of the future or the unknown. Simply, just being caught in the moment and focus on it. It's harder to achieve than it seems, though, but it's not impossible.

Just when I thought about letting my worries devour me and swallow my whole being while the real me is trapped inside, I had an odd dream which I knew meant something. In the dream, a figure was talking to me while I was in a cage made of white sticks; it was telling me to unlock the cage using the key I held on my chest. It just smiled, and I suddenly woke up. I recalled my dream and to my surprise, the key that the figure was trying to point, was actually my gold locket necklace with my picture in it when I was fifteen. Then I remembered that during those years, I started to establish bold life goals and envision myself as I accomplish those goals one at a time. At fifteen I was vigorous, fearless and hopeful. As I pass through the memory lane, I suddenly deciphered the meaning of my dream. The figure I saw was conveying a message to me - to fight my inner demons and let myself be free from it; to rediscover myself and let my wings unfold once again; reveal my true identity that lies inside of me. It might sound bizarre, but in all honesty, it did happen.

It is for this reason that I sought help from a trusted friend, and he suggested that I go through meditation. At first, it sounded a little old school; yet it sounds exactly what I needed at that particular moment. I studied about meditation and mindfulness; ran through several books, journals, online publications/articles and I personally asked my friend to help me. He referred me to his mom's friend, Robert, a 46-year old cheerful lad, who introduced me to the world of Yoga. There are a lot of meditation techniques on how mindfulness can be achieved. The best technique that I've found is Yoga – as based on my experience.

Robert is an active member of a yoga class in our neighborhood, and we shared meaningful conversations about life, I even told him almost everything about me and the whole time I was talking he was actively listening. He shared pieces of his life (which significantly left me in awe) as well as how Yoga helped him live a happy and contented life together with his family. He may stumble upon some challenges along the way, yet he never loses balance or loses his sight on the most important things. His personality oozes with unyielding optimism that's very contagious. When in doubt, he just takes a deep breath and silently drift away into the realm of serenity as his smile curves. Seeing him joyful and lively at his age made me the envy of him but in a good way. He became an inspiration to me and after a while of pondering on things I finally resolved to indulge in Yoga (probably one of the best decisions I ever made).

It may sound old school or traditional, yet after few weeks I already felt the immense change that took place. I felt as if I was touched spiritually – like my soul has been lifted from such heavy burden. I can breathe freely as I close my eyes and feel time pass. Every day I wake up, I feel much more alive, and there's an ample feeling of joy deep in my heart. Better things came into existence, and I never felt more alive.

Given this, I'd like to share relevant points and topics in this book in which I hope could be of great help to others who want to start a new track in the journey of life. It's never too late to let a new chapter of your being commence. This new chapter will offer you insights regarding Yoga, starting off from the very basic information that you have to know. Some may already know a lot, a thing or two and even if you don't have any idea at all, this will serve as your guide if you pursue this activity. Of course, it is unnecessary to learn everything in just one reading; you must take all the time that you need and as much as possible, enjoy yourself while you're reading this (take a sip of coffee if you'd like). If you found lessons that you've grasped, then take it with you and share it with others. It might enlighten them in some ways you'll never know.

In contrast to what most people believe in nowadays, Yoga is more than just an exercise. It's a gradual activity that is beneficial to your mind, body, and spirit. It takes time but it's an investment that will truly reward you with impressive results. Also, included in this book are the essentials that you'll be needing before you start Yoga and tips about routines as well as diet plans that work best for a tip-top shape body. You'll obtain benefits that Yoga could provide you, and if you're conscious about keeping a fit body and right weight, you'll find significant how-to information here. Also, best poses that are effective in losing weight can be found in this book. Every pose signifies a profound sense which you will come to understand more as you read along. Furthermore, you'll encounter formulas to fulfill happier and healthier life and how Yoga can greatly affect your standpoint or outlook in life. There's much more to learn and discover, and this book will walk you through to what lies ahead of you.

Yoga is just a piece of the puzzle, but once you have unraveled the secrets you hold within you, things will be exciting, and it will put things into perspective. Just don't forget to embody the teachings of Yoga – it's more than just a physical routine but a healing therapy. Once your wounds heal and scars fade away, ultimately you'll become a stronger person who will never back down from anything that life throws at you.

The main question is; how do I bring the practice of mindfulness into my daily life? The answer is simple: purpose. To be mindful of your emotions, you must be able to find purposefulness in your actions and experiences. You must actively shape your mind in order to be mindful, and we are here to show you a few different ways to get started.

Be in the Moment

We've all been in the moment when we let our emotions get the best of us. Whether you allow yourself to wallow in self-pity after a bad break up, get extremely pissed when you are stuck in traffic, fall into a depression, feel like seeking revenge, or even just simply are craving a chocolate chip cookie like crazy, these are ALL examples of allowing the mind to wander with negative thoughts and emotions. When we indulge our brains with these thoughts, you are reinforcing your emotions and causing self-harm to your being. The thing is, most of these emotions take place in the past and the future. You are allowing these emotions that no longer exist, bother you in the present. What we must remember is that the future is a fantasy until the moment arrives. The only moment that we can experience is the here and the now. Unfortunately, it is a moment that most of us tend to avoid because we are too concerned about the time surrounding the present. This is where mindfulness comes into play.

When you become mindful of your experiences and your emotions, you pull your conscious into the present. Now, this doesn't mean that you never have to think about the past or the future, but it does mean that we must be mindful of thinking about the past and the future. When you direct your awareness from thoughts of a different time and anchor yourself into the present moment, you can decrease negative emotions in your present life. By doing so, you can fall into a certain calmness and allow yourself to grow from these emotions.

Allow Yourself to be Non-judgmental

As we mentioned earlier, mindfulness is about living in the present moment and being as non-judgmental as possible. While in practice, mindfulness is a non-reactive state. By doing so, you must remind yourself that a certain experience isn't good or bad. Instead, you must become aware of the experience, take notice of them, and then let it go. By being mindful, this allows you not to get upset over an experience you do not want to be a part of. By being mindful, you accept the moment as it arrives and then allow it to pass and cease to exist. This way, it cannot negatively affect you. Whether it is pleasant or painful, you must treat each experience in the same manner.

Fixing your Thoughts and Conscious

Now that you understand that you must be mindful of your experiences, the question is, how can you fix your thoughts? Remember that while there are both pleasant and unpleasant experiences, you must remember to keep a certain stillness and a balance of your mind. You can do this by developing an acceptance in a friendly curiosity. The main purpose of mindfulness is to have this attitude of acceptance. By doing so, you get your thoughts away from pushing the experience away or clinging onto it. The first step of moving on from the moment is to fully recognize where you are, how you are feeling, and how to move on. For practice, try telling yourself: "It's okay," "Let me feel this," and "It is okay to feel this way." By repeating this to yourself, you are averting the negative emotions and creating a creative response to the situation. By telling yourself that the emotions you are feeling are acceptable, you can break out of the vicious cycle of feeling bad as we had mentioned earlier.

It is important to realize that to be healthy and mindful, you must have the ability to stand back from your thoughts and emotions whether they be negative or positive. You must consciously realize that the thoughts in your mind are not your true reality. When your thoughts begin to race, allow them to stream and then let them go. Remember that thoughts only occur if we put our time and energy into them. If you want to let go of the negative energy, you simply stop them from being created and create a space of freedom for yourself.

While it may seem complicated, letting go of your thoughts can be made easy. For some people, all it takes is simply labeling your thoughts as useful. Often, you may notice that you are thinking to yourself. When you find yourself deep in thought, try whispering the word "thinking" to yourself so that you can name your experience and then let it go and move on from the moment. If this doesn't work for you, try adapting to a skeptical attitude of your thoughts. At times, thoughts can either bring us down or empower us. Instead of instantly believing your thoughts, question your beliefs and then become aware that what you were thinking is only a thought. By doing so, this will also allow you to move on from the moment.

Some of us may need a bit more than just keeping our thoughts in and out of our brain. In the next few chapters, we will be discussing the benefits of both meditation and yoga for mindfulness. By bringing these practices into your daily life, you can become mindful and reap the benefits of practicing these relaxing exercises. We offer you the details of the practice and a step-by-step guide to getting you started. Our main goal is to help teach you how to become relaxed and live a healthier life. We hope you are enjoying the read so far. Stick around for the next chapter of Meditation for Mindfulness.

Chapter 20: Introducing The Concept Of Mindfulness

When you read the word Mindfulness, images of figures in orange robes contorting themselves into seemingly uncomfortable positions and chanting 'Om' likely comes to mind. Firstly, sorry, that is not what I intend for you. Unless you particularly want to go down that path (you know, your life – your journey), then please, go ahead. What I mean is, your approach to self-care, self-awareness, and your general presence 'at the moment'; the very facets of existence we seem to be overlooking in our everyday lives.

I recently came across an **excellent presentation** by Neuroscientist Sara Lazar who discusses her approach towards the concept of mindfulness and incorporating this into her life. As a skeptical academic who has since conducted validated research into this field, she is a leading example of how exploring the benefits and practices of mindfulness with an open mind can be worthwhile for you.

So, what is mindfulness?

Definitions of the term vary and often depend on context, however, a broad and relatively simple definition we will use is: Mindfulness is the psychological process of focusing your thoughts and energy on being fully present in a moment, applying self-awareness of your thoughts, bodily sensations environment and emotions while not becoming overwhelmed or particularly reactive in response. Thus, the definition is where most people fall. "Mindfulness means having to concentrate a lot, right?" Wrong. Concentrating too much can defeat the purpose and objective of your efforts, and you are likely leaning more towards the realm of being reflective or corrective – this can often spiral, and you may quickly find yourself berating your decisions or actions. To consider this more simply, mindfulness is savoring the taste of a moment, and appreciating the moment you are living in. In an era of recording moments through the screen of our smartphones, I can guarantee you, to fail to practice mindfulness is to live absently and with a risk of regret.

Another perhaps less acknowledged aspect of mindfulness is that of judgement. Once you enter a mindset of judgement, you immediately leave a mindful state and begin a negative comparative analysis. Here rings true the statement of "there are two sides to every story", and it is likely you are only exposed to one of those sides. In comparison, mindfulness encourages neutrality and acceptance.

The attitude of acceptance truly complements practices of mindfulness, in that mindful acceptance is an effective approach to dealing with negative emotions or resistance. Resistance may be considered as a complaint, and from a complaint there often rises tension between the individual and the moment's situation. When learning of and adopting an attitude of acceptance, it is critical to remember acceptance does not equate to resignation of the situation. Rather, acceptance can be considered more aligned to the process of acknowledgement, where a moment is noticed, observed and promotes awareness of the experience.

Practicing Acceptance

Please don't confuse the idea of practicing acceptance with the thought that you need to change your values or 'move the goalposts' as it were on certain matters. As I mentioned earlier, acceptance in this context can be likened more to that of a coping strategy rather than a decision-making tool.

Well, that's great, but where and how do I start?

Breathing.

Possibly our most basic human instinct and priority for living, breathing and the use of effective breathing methods can very easily help in reaching a state of acceptance. Better yet, breathing methods can be taught basically or in quite extensive detail depending on your level of interest and commitment to the mindfulness journey. Remember, acceptance is merely being rather than learning how to be. When negative emotions or resistance arise, your coping strategy of acceptance is to banish these thoughts. I do acknowledge some thoughts need dealing with; however, unless those thoughts pertain to that particular moment, then entertaining those thoughts serves no beneficial purpose to you in practicing mindfulness.

Before I continue, I want to make it clear: Banishing unproductive thoughts is not avoidance. The subconscious mind operates by memorizing actions that have developed into habits. Should those habits pertain to worrying about the past or the future, then they are fruitless habits that will not enhance your life or assist in developing you into a more mindful individual. If, however, you learn the habit of being mindful; instead, your mind is strengthened, your focus becomes more intense, and you are able to solve problems that may, at another time in your life, have seemed impossible. Mindfulness enables you to 'de-clutter' your thoughts and regain your focus – a practice we, as a millennial-dominated culture, seem to have forgotten.

Conclusion

The main aim of mindfulness meditation, as illustrated in this great eBook is for us to be able to slow down enough so that we can experience life to its fullest. It is not actually a means of staying away from the life's negative aspects, but rather to live those experiences so that we can learn how to cope with them in the best possible manner. Negativity is one thing that a number of us always try to avoid, yet find out that we may succeed when it comes to avoidance for a given time, but still discover that we are hit with what we have been trying to avoid all along.

What mindfulness does is to ask us to be fully aware of all our emotions, to be able to feel everything, including even the negativity. In doing that, we end up getting used with what we tried to avoid at first. If there is one thing that coping teaches us then it is dealing with the future negativity that are in our lives.

Mindfulness meditation can actually influence a number of things like the manner in which a person relates to his own feelings and thoughts. And in that same regard, it can still be seen as a healthy tool for general physical and emotional wellbeing.

Despite the tones of research that has been undertaken on this subject, researchers still caution those who want to make claims that meditation is one of the wonder drugs. In fact, they refer to this as taking at face value grandiose claims. Therefore, even if your practice of mindfulness meditation is not as evidence-based as you might have wanted it to be, it does not really have to be so that it can play an important and positive role in your own life

Living mindfully is a day-to-day practice of noticing some of the little things. For instance, one eats mindfully by doing that intentionally, and just savoring every bite, as opposed to rushing through a meal without really tasting the food. As you rush from one task to the other, or during your commute, you can intentionally or mindfully notice the hidden details of people, buildings, flora, and even the little cracks in the sidewalk.

But the question that always is how the entire process of mindfulness can really lead us to feeling peace within us. Here is the short answer to this question – the main aim of mindfulness is to make us live in the present. By control, a reference is made to our ability to change both our perceptions and thoughts. If we allow our thoughts to remain either in the future or in the present, we will suffer from anxiety and stress since we do not have control over those kind of time periods. All we can do from the past is just to learn the lessons that it offered. The future enables us to prepare in the present time for the unknown that might come any time. Thus, keeping the thoughts focused on the current moment enables us to experience and feel life to its fullest, while picking the thoughts that we wish to think.

Mindfulness has not just been effective over the centuries, but it has now been proven through a number of scientific researches that have been undertaken. It is a means of getting the inner peace that all of us are looking for.

www.ingramcontent.com/pod-product-compliance
Lightning Source LLC
Chambersburg PA
CBHW072014070526
44583CB00015B/1471